Price Guide to Vintage Coca-Cola Collectibles: 1896-1965

Deborah Goldstein Hill

Published by

krause
publications

700 E. State Street • Iola, WI 54990-0001
Telephone: 715/445-2214

Please, call or write us for our free catalog of antiques and collectibles publications.
To place an order or receive our free catalog, call 800-258-0929.

For editorial comment and further information,
use our regular business telephone at (715) 445-2214.

Library of Congress Catalog Number: 98-87356

ISBN: 0-87341-723-2

Printed in the United States of America

Dedication

I would like to dedicate this book to my husband and my daughter. Arthur has been by my side for the last 20 years. He helped me republish my parents' books 20 years ago. He went to conventions, auctions, swap meets, and even helped me when I wrote a column on Coca-Cola collectibles. Rebecca has been my light while I worked too many hours on the details of this book. She spent many hours sorting and cataloging photographs for me. I should mention that she is 13 and wanted to help her mom. She spent lots of time as a computer assistant running down lists to ensure our accuracy and reminded me how to do a bibliography.

Preface

My memories of Coca-Cola began when I was 12. My father became obsessed with his collection. Once he was bitten by the Coke bug, there was no turning back. He was working full-time on his collection, corresponding, buying and trading. It got to the point when he couldn't leave for fear he would miss a phone call. He was worried about insurance and security.

Everything that is in this book was in our elaborately decorated home to enhance the beautiful Coca-Cola girls. The house was a huge white colonial with white pillars and a circular driveway. Framed calendars adorned the spiral staircase. If you turned around, you would see the full-size Victorian-dressed mannequins. These women were artistic re-creations with authentic clothing, including hats, gloves and shoes.

The living room was the most beautiful and the most spectacular of his collection. All of the trays were exquisitely displayed with special lighting to enhance the colors. No one at this time had so many original and perfect trays. The curio cabinets held the most delicate and untouchable of collectibles, and these were always my most favorite. I had to visit them every now and then to see what had been the latest find. The knives and watch fobs were protected inside of glass-covered wall frames built especially for these special collectibles.

The guest bathroom was quite unusual, having been wallpapered professionally with old and original Coca-Cola color ads. The downstairs bar was the most colorful and fun for the family. of course, like any good Coca-Cola collectors, we had our vending machine stocked with 6-1/2 oz. bottles of cold Coke ready for any visitor. The bar was complete with many types of glasses and bottles. Signs everywhere, the Buddy Lee and Santa dolls displayed in their glass-covered houses and milk glass globes replaced normal fixtures. On the mantel was the beautiful dome clock. Coca-Cola was everywhere, from the krumkake maker in the kitchen, the Tiffany lamp in the dining room. Curio cabinets full of precious memorabilia was everywhere.

—*Deborah Goldstein-Hill*

Table of Contents

Introduction

Coca-Cola memorabilia is the most widely collected of all advertising memorabilia. It's little wonder when you consider the monumental quantity and beautiful quality of items produced. Coca-Cola advertising memorabilia provides an entertaining panorama of American history.

I've often wondered what it would be like to live in a time when Coca-Cola cost only a nickel, when gas was less than 25 cents a gallon, and a trip to the soda fountain was the main event of the day. It's a different world now. Ice-cold Coke now pops out of a talking vending machine that requires two quarters, and real soda fountains have become a rarity.

The Coca-Cola Company started by giving away the necessities—bottles, glasses and carriers. The company later adorned soda fountains with signs, clocks and trays. Fountain and store owners were given clocks, lamps and coolers to show appreciation for their loyalty. The individual bottlers provided toys, cars, knives, fans and playing cards to attract business. Coca-Cola felt that giving away gift premiums was a strategic way to increase its business.

This book has been prepared for all collectors of Coca-Cola. As we stand on the brink of the 21st century, this guide represents a century's worth of memories from the world's largest soft drink company.

I have every book on the subject of Coca-Cola. I appreciate the efforts of the Coca-Cola Company, the collectors and the researchers who have allowed us all to enjoy and share in the history. As a collector, or any person looking for knowledge, you should have all the books or information possible. It is not necessary to adopt just one person's opinion. It is best to gather lots of ideas and form your own opinion.

I took over the book publishing from my father in 1979. He had already sold his collection and was onto his next project. There was a huge demand for the books so they were republished in their exact form. These books were art books and collectors books—not necessarily just price guides. A few years later the Index to Coca-Cola Collectibles was published to further update the prices of the original books.

Over a period of eight years, I was very involved with the Coca-Cola Collector's Group. I went to Atlanta and met with the Coca-Cola Company. I was attending all the conventions, swap meets and auctions, in addition to writing a column to answer questions for collectors. At that time, I was receiving hundreds of letters a month.

In 1982, Wallace-Homestead published my next book, which took the four Coca-Cola Collectibles books and condensed them into a small easy-to-use compact reference book for identification and pricing. This book is a culmination of all my knowledge on the Coca-Cola Company's history and memorabilia. I started working on this book by simply doing an update with new prices. Instead, I got carried away with the fabulous story of our country's history that this company brings to us. It's fun and interesting to follow the historical tour back through the roots of America.

Starting a Collection

Collecting Coca-Cola memorabilia allows a collector a great freedom for expansion and a wide variety of categories from which to choose. A collector may already have Coke items within a pre-existing collection. For example, there are many people who collect toys and trucks who already have several Coca-Cola items and then take those items and branch off into Coca-Cola.

Other people like variety and collect every type of Coke item. I collect change trays and glass items, while my husband collects strictly signs. There are also people who specialize in a particular category of Coca-Cola memorabilia. There is a man in Kentucky who has acquired more than 100 different blotters during the last decade. I also see collectors who specialize in toys, trucks, bottles, paper items or signs.

In the early 1960s, my parents began collecting Vienna art plates (my father was attracted by the beautiful women that adorned them). While vacationing in California, my parents ran across their first old-fash-

Horse-drawn wagon delivers Coca-Cola.

Columbus, Ohio, Coca-Cola bottling plant.

ioned ice cream parlor. They reminisced as they viewed the many serving trays displayed. It was then they decided to build their own collection of Coca-Cola serving trays. They started searching antique stores, particularly those specializing in advertising antiques. They attended antique shows, auctions and flea markets. They read and placed ads in various trade papers. Of greatest significance, my father began to correspond daily with collectors around the world.

In the beginning stages of collecting, my father bought every item that was available. I think he feared that he would not see another. As he became more experienced, he began to upgrade his collection so that it included only items in mint condition. By 1972, he had the largest and most complete collection of serving trays in the country, and it included two one-of-a-kind trays.

It was at this point that they began to catalog their trays known as "Betty," "Elaine" and "Lillian." With the beautiful photographs and indexing complete, a book seemed the natural next step. In 1972, Shelly and Helen Goldstein introduced Coca-Cola Collectibles Volume I in Indianapolis at the first Advertising Antique Show. Because of the size and beauty of their collection, they were able to prepare a book each year after that. As the Philadelphia Inquirer of 1975 stated simply: "These books stimulated wider interest in collecting Coca-Cola items."

When Shelly and Helen began producing their books in 1970, very little information had been gathered. The Coca-Cola Company had not yet gotten involved with collectors, and there was no formal group or newsletter. There were only a handful of enthusiasts who energized the world of Coca-Cola collectibles, and Shelly and Helen were definitely on that list. Their books were beautifully produced and still today are one of the best displays in full color of Coca-Cola memorabilia. For some, these books are the only way to view such a beautiful collection.

Wilbur Kurtz, the archivist for Coca-Cola at the time, has been known to spin some tales from the chronicles of Coca-Cola. He was the only contact Shelly had with Coca-Cola at the time. Apparently, there have been some discrepancies that I am attempting to correct in this book. The obvious one that I have heard so much about is mistaking Lillian Russell for Lillian Nordica, and we now know that Lillian Nordica was the first model for Coca-Cola. The next issue has to do with the dating of calendars and other items. We assumed that the date for a calendar was its copyright date, which is printed on the left bottom corner of a calendar. The collector date, is actually considered the year of the artwork's first use—in other words, the copyright date for the artwork. If there is no calendar pad, dating would be difficult as one would assume to use the date printed on the calendar.

Tips for Buying & Selling

Treasure Hunting at Swap Meets: If you are attending a swap meet go early. If you are a dealer with a booth to set up, you usually only have one hour to set up, so keep your booth's design simple. As soon as you begin to unpack, you will find people roaming around to see what's around the next corner—be ready. Much of the selling and trading is done before the doors ever open.

There is always a lot of activity at a swap meet. Be careful about buying a questionable item. Use your book to identify the items and compare prices. Talk about your purchase with others (most dealers like to show their expertise). There are always people who bring items to trade with dealers. Sometimes they have an item that you have been wanting for a long time. This is a good chance to make a swap.

Swap meets are exciting and there are so many opportunities to meet new friends. Buy anything that suits your fancy. As long as it displays the familiar Coca-Cola trademark, it's collectible!

Auctions: Auctions are fast-paced and high-energy events. I have brought home some true finds from auctions. I have also bought things that I wouldn't normally buy and possibly overpaid for certain items. There is always an auction preview. This is where bidders have a chance to view the merchandise and note the identification number of the items they intend to bid on. Once the auctioneer begins, it is time to pay attention.

"Going once. Going twice. Going three times. Sold for $250." To you? Maybe. If it seems frightening, start by bidding very low, as close to the original bid as possible. On the fourth or fifth bid, sit back and you will be outbid. This will give you some practice. If you want the item, bid for it. Don't forget that payment is required at the auction's close.

Internet: A relatively new phenomenon is buying and selling over the Internet, either through on-line auctions (such as ebay.com) or from companies or individual sellers. This mode of collecting will undoubtedly become a bigger marketplace in the future. To avoid pitfalls of buying and selling on the 'net, know how to buy and sell and know who you're buying and selling from.

Grading the Condition

Special Rare Class: Items pre-1904 fall into this classification.

Mint: New condition, in original unused state, no visible marks.

Near-mint: a classification into which most items that are thought of as mint, would fall. Not in original mint condition. Close inspection would reveal very minor or slight marks of age or use.

Excellent: Only minor, hairline-type scratches visible without close examination. Small chip, chips, or marks on outer rim or edge of item.

Very Good: Minor surface scratch or scratches. Rust spots of no more than pinhead size. Minor flaking. Picture, lettering and color in excellent condition.

Good: Minor scratch or scratches, minor flaking, minor fading, possibly minor dents. Little rust or pitting.

Fair: Major scratch or scratches on surface. Picture or lettering faded. Rust spots on surface. Minor dent or dents. Bad chipping or flaking on surface.

Poor: Badly rusted, worn, dented, pitted, torn, not repairable.

Pricing

The most practical basis for pricing would seem to be what someone is willing to pay vs. how much someone wants for an item. Without getting into the philosophy of sales, I can safely say that some Coke enthusiasts have no basis for what they are willing to pay.

While attending an auction, I talked with a woman who had been working on her Coca-Cola toy collection for years. She searched for five years until she finally found the 1938 toy stove. I feel the basis for her purchase must have been what she was willing and able to afford, vs. how much the dealer needed to sell his treasure. I thought she overpaid, if she wanted to recoup it in reselling the item. However, she felt she would never resell and was willing to pay any price. Her toy stove has more than tripled in value in the last 10 years.

In The Classic Collector, spring 1974, my father was quoted as saying, "When I first started collecting Coke items eight years ago, people were complaining that prices were too high. Five years from now, today's prices will look cheap in comparison."

My pricing system is designed with averages in mind. While someone might pay an outrageous price for a key collectible, it is not considered its worth. But what about one-of-a-kind items? When my father sold his collection to the Schmidt Museum, they could afford to pay and needed to pay top dollar for pieces that would make their collection one-of-a-kind. So one expensive piece could actually raise the value of an entire collection.

At the time Shelly and Helen were collecting, they had the means to pay whatever it took to expand their collection. They started by purchasing anything and trading up from there. Even after my father had a mint piece, he would continue to buy everything he could. If you are trading, it is effective because an item can be more valuable to another collector than money.

I think it is wonderful to collect any and all parts of Coca-Cola collectibles. I don't think it is necessary to collect only vintage stuff. When people were collecting in the late 1960s, the items from the '60s were not considered highly collectible at the time. However, those collectibles have gone up in value considerably over the years.

I suggest collecting anything that makes you happy, piques your interest and excites you—that's what it's all about. I love the Coca-Cola collectibles from the '60s and '70s, and these items are escalating in value as new things are manufactured. During the 1990s, Coca-Cola has delved full force into licensing, and there are many delightful new categories of bright fun things to collect.

My daughter and her friends are not interested in the old collectibles. They are from a different generation that wants to see colorful, noisy, whimsical and entertaining collectibles. They enjoy the clothes, jewelry, toys and dolls. I suggest collecting things your children enjoy, so when they grow up they will have the collectibles of the future.

Important People of Coca-Cola

John Styth Pemberton: In the spring of 1886, John Styth Pemberton was cooking up the first batch of what was to become Coca-Cola. Mixing the syrup in a three-legged kettle in the backyard of his Atlanta home, Pemberton experimented with what he foresaw as a headache remedy and "tonic stimulant." Clearly, John Pemberton could not have known that his formula would become the base of the world's most popular soft drink.

Born in 1831 in Knoxville, Ga., Pemberton grew up and was educated in Columbus, Ohio. Part of his education consisted of an apprenticeship in pharmaceuticals. After the Civil War, Pemberton moved to Atlanta, where he established himself as a druggist and pharmaceutical chemist. He became known for his original compounds advertised as health supplements and cures for various common ailments. Indeed, the precursor to Coca-Cola was a mixture designed to cure headaches. He sold his patent medicines as Globe Flower Cough Syrup, Extract of Stillingia, Tuplix Liver Pills and Lemon & Orange Elixir.

Pemberton patented his mixture in 1885 and called it Pemberton French Wine of Coca. Atlanta became a dry town in 1886. By taking out the wine and adding extract of cola and other ingredients, Pemberton formulated an as yet unnamed syrup. This syrup eventually became the base of the now famous Coke. Pemberton's formula, which contained caffeine from the cola nut, was promoted as a remedy for nervous disorders and stomach upset. Sugar was added to the syrup to mask the bitter taste and citric acid added to balance the sweetness of the sugar.

Shortly after its creation in May of 1886, Pemberton took a jug of his new syrup to Willis Venable, the manager of the largest soda fountain in Atlanta. Venable liked the taste when he mixed the syrup with water and agreed to sell the drink at his soda fountain. A few months later, the story has it, a new soda clerk accidentally mixed the syrup with soda water. During this time, soda fountains were growing in popularity. They were dispensing soda water, root beer, phosphates and other flavored drinks.

The name Coca-Cola was given to the drink after its popularity had grown. The name was chosen as an appealing alliterative combination of the drink's two ingredients. Although ill health soon forced Pemberton to sell his rights to his new product, the special blend of ingredients basically has remained unchanged. Pemberton died in August of 1888 without seeing the complete success of his creation, but it is certain that he knew something of the drink's value.

Asa Candler: Frank Robinson was trying to sell Asa Candler a printing machine, when Robinson and David Doe were sold on Pemberton's newly developed elixir. It was Robinson that placed the first ad in the Atlanta Daily Journal. He took over the daily management of the company. Somehow, Robinson lost his stake in the product and soon found Asa Candler to buy the outstanding stock from Pemberton. Robinson continued to work for Candler after he took over the company.

On Aug. 30, 1888, two weeks after the death of John S. Pemberton, Asa Griggs Candler acquired the remaining one third of Coca-Cola stock for a mere $1,000. Candler had become the controlling owner in

Coca-Cola delivery truck.

the months prior to Pemberton's death, and these final steps made him Coca-Cola's sole proprietor. Candler had spent $2,300 on the rights to the soft drink that he would soon lead from obscurity to national prominence.

Candler was born on Dec. 30, 1851, near Villa Rica, Ga. Although the Civil War had disrupted his education and had left him with only seven years of formal schooling, Candler became an apprentice to Dr. Best and Dr. Carter of Cartersville, Ga., at the age of 19. While he was unable to achieve his dream of becoming a doctor, Candler was able to amass a working knowledge of pharmaceuticals and become a pharmacist.

In 1873, he moved to Atlanta where he put his knowledge to work at the Pemberton-Pulliam Drug Store. After building up a reputation and some capital, Candler and a partner started their own retail and wholesale drug business. The business suffered when their building was destroyed by fire. They purchased Pemberton, Iverson and Denison, a drug company with which they could service their accounts. His list of proprietary medicines included Electric Bitters, Everlasting Cologne, Botanic Blood Balm and De-Lec-Ta-Lave. By 1888, Candler led the largest drug store in Atlanta.

Soon, Candler became the sole owner of the company, and he acquired the exclusive rights to Coca-Cola in August 1888. In 1889, Candler published his first full-page advertisement in the Atlanta Journal promoting his product as "Delicious, Refreshing, Exhilarating, Invigorating." He was also distributing thousands of coupons for a free glass of his product. He further promoted Coca-Cola by putting the name on everything and giving it away. Realizing its potential, Candler dropped all of his other products to concentrate on the soft drink. In 1903, Candler removed the cocaine, knowing of its addictive properties. Pemberton's original syrup had remained basically unchanged. The decision proved to be a profitable one, as the company showed a $100,000 gross profit each of its first two years.

In 1892, Candler, along with Frank Robinson (his brother) and two associates, incorporated the Coca-Cola Company. In 1895, the trademark Coca-Cola was registered with the U.S. Patent Office. Candler moved his Coca-Cola business to Atlanta. In succeeding years, Coca-Cola expanded enormously. The first syrup manufacturing plants were opened in Dallas, Chicago and Los Angeles. In 1909, the Atlanta operation moved into a huge, new building at the corner of Marietta and Magnolia Streets.

Candler stepped down as president of the company in 1916. It's obvious that his strength and dedication started Coca-Cola on its path toward success. During his reign, Coca-Cola became one of the most successful businesses in the country. In 1919, Candler sold his company to the Trust Company of Georgia, which was led by Ernest Woodruff. Times were changing. Now, whether you wanted to order one at the fountain or drink it from a bottle, all things were possible.

Robert Woodruff: In a few years, Robert Woodruff took over the company from his father, as he was elected president of the company. He saw the potential of bottling; by 1928, bottle sales took the lead over fountain sales. We would rarely think today of buying a single bottle of Coke—however, until 1920, a six-pack had not been pioneered. a simple merchandising tool, the cardboard carton, became a "home package with a handle of invitation," a boost to the industry. The 1929 ad read, "Easy to buy. Easy to Carry. Easy to keep on Ice. With a six box on hand, you are always prepared for wholesome refreshment—for your family and unexpected guests—for bridge parties, luncheons and picnics." The next advance became the open-top cooler which allowed an ice cold bottled Coca-Cola to be served in a retail environment. The cold taste of Coke could be had at the workplace or while shopping. The original red and green rolling coolers made ice cold Coca-Cola available to weary travelers on the road.

Soda fountains had been dispensing Coke manually since its inception. The 1933 Chicago World's Fair was the introduction of the automatic fountain dispenser where flavor and soda water could be poured and mixed as one. The dispenser was developed by the Dole Valve Company of Chicago. It measured the correct amount of syrup and then mixed it with carbonated water. They were amazed as the server pulled a handle to dispense their favorite drink. By 1937, the automatic dispenser became the norm in the soda fountain setting. In the early years, Candler managed to get the syrup to Cuba

1910 photo of the Coca-cola Convention in Atlanta.

and Puerto Rico. In 1939, one-gallon syrup cans were made to ship syrup. Syrup distribution began also in Panama and the Philippines as bottling operations were built internationally. In 1920, France became the first European bottler of Coca-Cola. This was the beginning as Woodruff set off to bring Coca-Cola to every corner of the world.

While Coca-Cola was already being bottled in 44 countries, World War II presented new challenges for Woodruff. He ordered that "every man in uniform gets a bottle of Coca-Cola for 5c, wherever he is and whatever it costs the company." Along with dispensed Coke from mobile units, 5 billion bottles of Coca-Cola were consumed by military personnel. In 1943, he mandated that 10 new bottling plants be shipped and constructed as close to fighting areas in Europe and the Pacific. More than just giving the troops the taste they had grown to love, they gave many their first taste of this most popular drink. They actually built 64 new bottling plants, and the close of the war brought huge growth to the company.

Joseph Biedenharn: In the first years of Coca-Cola's existence, the popular beverage could be found only at the local soda fountain. It was not until the summer of 1894 that Joseph Biedenharn began to bottle Coke, the soft drink that was selling so well in his Vicksburg, Miss., store. He was so impressed with the drink that he decided to use his bottling equipment to bottle Coke in the rear of his store.

Biedenharn, a native of Vicksburg, Miss., was born Dec. 13, 1866. As a teenager, he joined his father's firm, which sold fruit, nuts and candies. Eventually, he took over the company and moved it into a large building in Vicksburg. The success of his business allowed him to run both a retail candy shop/soda fountain, as well as a wholesale candy and nut warehouse. In 1890, a Coca-Cola salesman persuaded Biedenharn to offer Coke at his soda fountain.

The Biedenharn Candy Company began bottling soda water in 1891, and three years later, the company introduced Coke by the bottle. The idea behind the innovation was to make Coke available to people who did not live near soda fountains. Soon, Biedenharn was delivering bottled Coca-Cola throughout the Vicksburg area and by boat up and down the Mississippi River. When he died in 1952, Joseph Biedenharn had been a Coca-Cola bottler for 58 years. Since Coca-Cola was not originally created to be sold as a bottled soft drink, the founders could not have perceived enormous potential in bottling their beverage.

Biedenharn was already bottling other drinks when he began bottling Coke. Bottles were used interchange-

ably, so the first Coke bottles did not bear the drink's distinctive logo. The original Coke bottle had a 6 oz. capacity and cost 70 cents for a case wholesale (compared to 60 cents for a case of regular soda water). The short, 6 oz. bottles used the popular Hutchinson stopper. This type of bottle top was rather bulky and consisted of a rubber gasket held between two metal plates attached to a spring wire stem. The bottles were identified only by embossments "Registered" and "Biedenharn Candy Co., Vicksburg, Miss." In 1897, the second bottler to put carbonated Coca-Cola in bottles was the Valdosta (Georgia) Bottling Works owned by R.H. Holmes and E.R. Barber. Their Hutchinson-stopper bottles were marked "Valdosta Electric Bottling Works, Valdosta, Ga." Like the Biedenharn bottles, they were not marked, "Coca-Cola."

In 1899, Candler gave Benjamin F. Thomas and Joseph B. Whitehead exclusive rights to bottle Coca-Cola in the entire United States, except for the territories covered by pre-existing contracts in the New England states, Mississippi and Texas. These two men convinced Candler that they would deliver Coca-Cola to people everywhere by building plants and bottling Coke. In 1899, the first Coca-Cola Bottling plant opened in Chattanooga, Tenn. That opening was followed a year later by Atlanta's first Coca-Cola bottling plant. Distribution grew as local bottlers invested in their business in exchange for exclusive rights to bottle and distribute Coca-Cola within a specified territory. This brilliant idea spurred their success.

One of the central problems in the bottling industry before the turn-of-the-century was finding a suitable bottle closure. There were hundreds invented during this period, including the Hutchinson stopper, but none were completely without problems. The main objection to the Hutchinson top was the fact that its rubber gasket became odorous and unsanitary if the bottle was not opened in about two weeks.

William Painter: In 1891, William Painter of Baltimore invented what was to become the most practical and popular bottle top of the first half of the 20th century—the crown cork. Although Coca-Cola did not make the crown cork mandatory with its bottlers until the emergence of its standardized bottle in 1916, this bottle closure marked an era of new sophistication in the bottling industry. Bottles during this crown cork-era were marked by the trademark Coca-Cola on the bottle, bottle cap or on a paper label attached to the side of the bottle. The earliest bottles used for Coca-Cola contained only the syrup, not the carbonated beverage we know today. John Pemberton used plain bottles with paper labels marked, "Coca-Cola Syrup and Extract" to distribute the syrup to soda fountains.

Advertising Is It!

By the immediate familiarity of the following phrases, "The Pause That Refreshes," "It's The Real Thing!" and "Things Go Better With Coke!," it is clear that the promotion and advertising of Coca-Cola has been enormously successful. And, although John Styth Pemberton's syrup makes an undeniably great beverage, quality advertising has been a major force in turning Coca-Cola into the world's most popular soft drink. The success can be attributed in part to the advertising principles initiated over 75 years ago by Asa Candler and W. C. D'Arcy. In 1929, "The Pause that Refreshes" first appeared in the Saturday Evening Post.

Since the first Coca-Cola advertisements of the 1880s and 1890s, beautiful and elegant men and women have been shown in settings that the public admires and aspires toward. In its advertising, Coca-Cola has presented itself as standing for quality, decency, wholesomeness and, most importantly, the American lifestyle. Coca-Cola has always aligned itself with the goodness of America and its people. These principles are clearly seen even in the first lithographs of pretty, wholesome girls drinking Coke from Asa Candler's era. By the century's end, however, that medium was becoming obsolete and four-color advertisements were present in magazines. At that point, Candler decided to hand the growing task of representation over to the Massengale Advertising firm.

Massengale took over the advertising for Coca-Cola in the early 1900s, but its tenure was short-lived and its advertising pieces are now considered rare. In general, the firm's advertisements showed beautiful people drinking Coke and playing what were then the sports of the rich—tennis, golf and swimming.

In 1906, W.C. D'Arcy became Coca-Cola's advertising agency. Idea man Archie Lee and Coca-Cola President Robert Woodruff developed and produced ideas and copy that conveyed the image for clean Americana in the tradition that Asa Candler had begun. The look was generally the same, with wholesome and active men and women. The focus of the D'Arcy advertisements began to shift subtly towards the growing middle class. Their ideas were simple, always associating Coca-Cola with pleasant surroundings.

By 1920, the Model T was everywhere and the roadside was the newest canvas to display the Coca-Cola message. Full color billboards and illuminated signs were added to the outdoor advertising campaign.

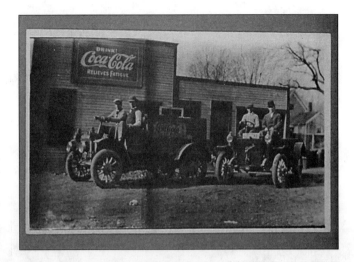

Delivering Coca-cola in 1909.

After Woodruff and Lee retired, Coca-Cola changed advertising agencies. McKann-Ericson, which is still Coke's advertising agency today, was chosen in 1956. The song, "I'd Like to Buy the World a Coke," was written by McKann-Ericson's Bill Backer. In the annual report of 1982, Coca-Cola states, "The Company's most successful advertising campaign ever developed for Coca-Cola—Coke is it!—achieved record consumer awareness."

In 1983, the company introduced the most significant product addition in 96 years, Diet Coke—a collaboration of the world-renown trademark with a great tasting, low-calorie soda.

Famous Coca-Cola Artists

Coca-Cola has become highly collectible not only for its variety of items, but also because of the beautiful artwork the company used to advertise its product. The artwork produced for Coca-Cola is a combination effort by the advertising agency, the artist and a writer.

In today's world, artist's compilation books are sent to each ad agency with pages of art representative of each artist's style. Back then, artist's books were not available. They used several of the same artists over periods of time. These artists were commissioned by the ad agency, not Coca-Cola. There were also stock artists, who were brought in after the original artwork was done, to add the Coke bottle or something specific they specialized in. My favorite artists for Coca-Cola were: Norman Rockwell, N.C. Wyeth, Frederic Stanley and Haddon Sundblom.

Like any advertising art today, product art is rarely, if ever, signed by the artist. Many of the artists on the following list were never famous, but simply completed their commissioned artwork on time and with the specifications that allowed it to be used. Artwork of any type is highly collectible. It does not need to be signed or in finished form. It could be sketches, comps or the artwork with or without print. A piece of art that would be used later in advertising Coca-Cola would be a very sought after collectible.

Notable Coca-Cola artists include: Harry Anderson, McClelland Barclay, Lester Beall, Joseph Binder, Al Buell, Pruet Carter, Dean Cornwell, Bradshaw Crandall, Stevan Dohanoe, Albert Dorne, Harvey Dunn, Gilbert Elvgren, A.T. Farrell, Fred Fixler, James Montgomery Flagg, Frank Godwin, Bill Gregg, Hananiah Harari, Charles Heizerling, John Held Jr., Everett Henry, John Howard, John Newton Howitt, Nick Hufford, Lynn Bogue Hunt, Gerald Keane, Hamilton King, B. Lichtman, Victor Livoti, Andrew Loomis, Athos Menaboni, Fred Mizen, Norman Price, George Rapp, Redoute, Norman Rockwell, Virgil Ross, George Schreiber, Lyman Simpson, Robert Skemp, Ben Stahl, Frederic Stanley, Haddon Sundblum, Kenneth Thompson, Larry Tisdale, Thorton Utz, L. Wilbur, Mortimer Wilson, Jack Witrup and N.C. Wyeth.

Acknowledgments

I would like to thank my mom, Gail Abbott, for her inspiration and confidence in me. I want to thank my sister, Lesa Angelo, who has been a good friend to me when I needed one the most. Thank you to Nannette Troutman for her love and support over the last several years. Thank you to my whole family: my brothers, Michael and Steven, my sisters, Jeni, Lesa and Ele, and my parents, Shelly and Helen Goldstein. Coca-Cola is synonymous with family and fun. We six children shared our home and our parents with Lillian, Hilda, Betty, Elaine, the Sprite Boy and all the delightful and fascinating wonders of the Coca-Cola Company.

Kudos to Bob Buffaloe for creating the first Coca-Cola Club for all the crazy zany Coca-Cola fanatics. Thank you to Alan Petretti for his continued work in the field of Coca-Cola collectibles.

Warning! To LKS

When I am an old woman, I shall wear purple
With a red hat that doesn't go, and doesn't suit me
And I shall spend my money on brandy and summer gloves
And satin sandals, and say we've got no money for butter.
I shall sit on the pavement when I'm tired
And gobble up all the samples in shops and press alarm bells
And run my stick along public railings
And make up for the sobriety of youth.
I shall go out in my slippers in the rain
And pick the flowers in other people's gardens
And learn to spit.

You can wear terrible shirts and grow more fat
And eat three pounds of sausages at a go
Or only bread and pickle for a week
And hoard pens and pencils and beermats
And things in boxes

But now we must have clothes that keep us dry
And pay our rent and not swear in the street
And set a good example for children
We must have friends to dinner and read the papers

But maybe I ought to practise a little now?
So people who know me
Are not too shocked and surprised
When suddenly I am old, and start to wear purple

Jenny Joseph

Deborah Goldstein Hill (right) with her daughter, Rebecca.

Price & Identification Guide

Blotters

Blotters were very popular during the first half of the century since dip pens and ink were used daily. Throughout the years, blotters have kept their basic oblong shape. Slogan changes are significant because they depict the energy of the times. From 1927 to 1935, blotters artwork mimicked billboard artwork. Many collectible blotters can be identified simply by the phrase written across the front.

Item	Value
1901, Coca-Cola, Delicious-Refreshing	$225.00
1904, Atlanta Litho & Print Co.	$1,000.00
1904, Delicious-Refreshing	$500.00
1904, Edwards Deutsch & Heitmann, Chicago	$450.00
1904, Atlanta Litho & Print Co.	$500.00
1904, No Litho Co.	$450.00
1905, Drink a Bottle of Carbonated Coca-Cola	$150.00
1905, The Most Refreshing Drink in the World	$150.00
1906, Strengthens the Nerves	$150.00
1906, Pure And Healthful	$125.00
1909, The Most Refreshing Drink in the World	$225.00
1909, Pure And Healthful	$125.00
1910, Absolutely Sanitary	$350.00
1911, Blue & Pink Backs	$900.00
1912, Pure And Healthful, Delicious & Refreshing	$125.00

Item	Value
1913, Delicious And Refreshing (two bottles)	$40.00
1913, Pure and Healthful Drink, Coca-Cola, Delicious-Refreshing	$40.00
1916, Made to Chew	$800.00
1916, Pure and Healthful Drink, Coca-Cola, Delicious-Refreshing	$30.00

1905, Drink a Bottle of Carbonated Coca-Cola—$150

1901, Coca-Cola, Delicious-Refreshing—$225

1913, Pure and Healthful Drink, Coca-Cola, Delicious-Refreshing—$40

1904, Delicious-Refreshing—$500

1916, Pure and Healthful Drink, Coca-Cola, Delicious-Refreshing—$3

1920s, set of six—$300

1929, A Pure Drink of Natural Flavors—$150

1929, The Pause That Refreshes—$100

Item	Value
1920s, set of six	$300.00
1920, Delicious-Refreshing (two fountain spigots)	$125.00
1923, Delicious And Refreshing (two glasses)	$400.00
1927, Coca-Cola	$60.00
1928, Coca-Cola—Refresh Yourself	$75.00
1929, Drink Coca-Cola-Delicious and Refreshing	$225.00
1929, The Pause That Refreshes	$100.00
1929, Wholesome Refreshment	$125.00
1929, A Pure Drink of Natural Flavors	$150.00

Item	Value
1929, The Pause That Refreshes	$100.00
1930, The Pause That Refreshes (woman)	$65.00
1930, The Pause That Refreshes (man)	$75.00
1930, The Pause That Refreshes	$75.00
1930, The High Sign of Refreshment	$175.00
1930, Off to a Fresh Start	$125.00
1931, Pure as Sunlight	$225.00
1931, Tune in Every Wednesday Night	$125.00
1931, Natural Refreshment	$100.00
1932, The Pause That Refreshes	$100.00
1932, Just To Remind You	$225.00
1932, ???	$225.00
1934, ???	$100.00
1934, A Natural Partner	$100.00
1934, ???	$100.00
1934, Coca-Cola	$100.00
1935, A Homerun With Three On	$60.00
1935, Carry a Smile Back To Work	$35.00
1935, Good With Food—Try It	$35.00
1935, The Drink That Keeps You Feeling Right	$45.00
1936, Fiftieth Anniversary 1886-1936	$50.00

1930, The Pause That Refreshes (woman)—$65

1930, The Pause That Refreshes (man)—$75

1941, The Pause That Refreshes—$85

Item	Value	Item	Value
1937, Cool Refreshment	$30.00	1944, How About a Coke	$15.00
1938, Any Time is the Right Time	$25.00	1945, Passport To Refreshment	$15.00
1938, Stop for a Pause—Go Refreshed	$20.00	1946, How About a Coke	$35.00
1939, The Drink Everybody Knows	$25.00	1947, Coke Knows No Season	$15.00
1940-50s, Canada	$30.00	1951, Delicious and Refreshing	$15.00
1940, Bring in Your Thirst And Go	$20.00	1952, 50th Anniversary	$100.00
1940, The Greatest Pause on Earth	$65.00	1950, Be Prepared—Be Refreshed	$15.00
1941, The Pause That Refreshes	$85.00	1953, Sprite Boy, "Good"	$15.00
1942, Completely Refreshed	$15.00	1956, Friendliest Drink on Earth	$15.00
1942, I Think It's Swell	$6.00	1957, Good	$20.00
1942, Refreshment That Can't Be Duplicated	$20.00	1957, 58 Million a Day	$12.00
1942, Wholesome Refreshment	$6.00	1960, Over 60 Million a Day	$12.00
1943, A Taste All It's Own	$15.00		

1946, How About a Coke—$35

1953, Sprite Boy, "Good"—$15

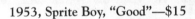

1947, Coke Knows No Season—$15

1956, Friendliest Drink on Earth—$15

Books

Item	Value
1916, *The Romance of Coca-Cola* (describes history of Coca-Cola through 1916)	$85.00
1923, *Facts*	$75.00
1928, *Alphabet Book of Coca-Cola*	$75.00
1928, *The 5 Star Book*	$40.00
1932, *When You Entertain*	$12.00
1939, *My Daily Reminder*	$15.00
1940, *The Red Barrel*	$15.00

1923, **Facts**—$75

1916, *The Romance of Coca-Cola* (describes history of Coca-Cola through 1916)—$85

1928, *Alphabet Book of Coca-Cola*—$75

Coke ABCs

The *ABC Book of Coca-Cola* is still one of my favorite pieces. The pages are pastel paintings of Coke being made or enjoyed. It combines each letter of the alphabet with Coca-Cola facts written in a poem, which follows:

A is for Alphabet/With which is told/The tale of the drink/That delights young and old

B is for Bottle/Baseball and bat!/Without Coca-Cola/The game would fall flat

C is for Cooling/"Served icy-cold"/The drink they all order/At the famed nineteenth hole

D for Delicious/The drink the world favors/Because it's a blend/Of nature's pure flavors

E—Effervescent/Sparkling and clear/Eight million served/Each day in a year

F is for Five cents/A popular price/You can always afford/To keep plenty on ice

G is for Good/A fact you can't quiz/It had to be good/To get where it is

H is for Home/Where this drink's a treat/Indeed, it's the thing/That makes home sweet home sweet

I—Invitation/Which the little red sign/Flashes so clearly/You cannot decline

J is for Journey/Tourists all say/"As you travel along/Be refreshed by the way"

K is for Kitchen/With ice box near by/If you keep Coca-Cola/You'll never go dry

L is for Lunch/You will find it if you try/With hot food or cold/A refreshing diet

M for the Maker/So careful and sure/That each bottle reaches/You wholesome and pure

N is for Now/Daytime or night/At any old time/You'll find it just right

O is for Order/And lest you forget it/The sooner you order/The sooner you'll get it

P is for Purity/Goodness sublime/"Round the corner from anywhere"/Any old time

Q is for Quality/Sure to be high and always the same/Wherever you buy

R is for Refresh Yourself/Hot days or cold/From Cuba to Canada, Millions are sold

S is for Stop/At the red sign so famed/All like to stop when/Coca-Cola is named

T is for Taste/Refreshing and fine/In this drink so delicious/For your thirst and mine

U is for Unanimous/Just hear what they say/When they want a cold drink/Any hot summer day

V is for Value/Though the dollar's depressed/A nickel still buys/The drink that's best

W—The Wide World/East, west, north or south/Is never in danger/Of suffering drought

X is for Xmas/When St. Nick comes down/He finds he can get it/In every town

Y is for You/If you've never tasted/This marvelous drink/Your taste has been wasted

Z is for Zest/There is no denying/Send for a case/It's surely worth trying

1939, *My Daily Reminder*—$15

1928, *The 5 Star Book*—$40

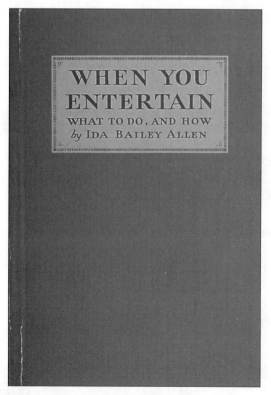

1932, *When You Entertain*—$12

1940, *The Red Barrel*—$15

The following books, given to U.S. soldiers, kept our fighting men and women current on important events.

Item	Value
1940, *Home and Flowers* by Laura Burroughs	$8.00
1940, *Flowering Arranging*	$10.00
1940, *Flower Arranging No. 2*	$8.00
1944, *The Coca-Cola Bottler*	$25.00

Item	Value
1943, *War Planes*	$45.00
1946, *Our America*	$5.00

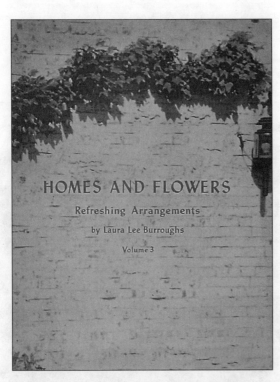

1940, *Home and Flowers* by Laura Burroughs—$8

1940, *Flower Arranging No. 2*—$8

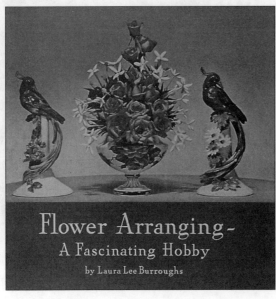

1940, **Home and Flowers by Laura Burroughs—$8**

1944, *The Coca-Cola Bottler*—$25

1943, War Planes—$45

1946, Our America—$5

The following books were distributed to our schools.

Item	Value
1957, Easy Hospitality	$5.00
1961, Pause for Living	$20.00
1961, Pause for Living, bound volume	$12.00

1957, *Easy Hospitality*—$5

1961, *Pause for Living*—$20

1961, *Pause for Living*—$20

Bookmarks

Item	Value	Item	Value
1896, Celluloid (back)	$1,000.00	1902, Hilda Clark	$425.00
1896, Celluloid, front)	$1,000.00	1903, Lillian Nordica, 6" x 2"	$425.00
1898, Celluloid, 2" x 2-1/4"	$425.00	1904, Lillian Russell	$525.00
1899, Celluloid	$550.00	1906, Owl	$825.00
1900, Hilda Clark	$725.00	1908, Coca-Cola Chewing Gum, 2" x 6"	$2,000.00

1896, Celluloid (back)—$1,000

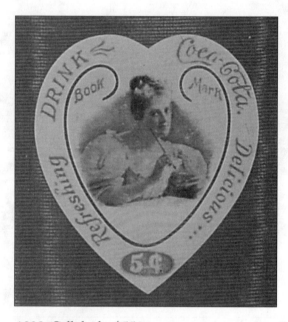

1899, Celluloid—$550

1896, Celluloid (front)—$1,000

1898, Celluloid, 2" x 2-1/4"—$425

1900, Hilda Clark—$725

1903, Lillian Nordica, 6" x 2"—$425

1898, Celluloid, 2" x 2-1/4"— $700

1904, Lillian Russell—$325

1906, Owl—$825

1908, Coca-Cola Chewing Gum, 2" x 6"—$2,000

The first advertising artwork printed on a bottle appeared in 1903. They were clear straight-sided bottles with diamond-shaped labels that were glued to the bottles. Much of the advertising items have been produced in two versions: one for fountain and one for bottles. To help combat the imitators, Coca-Cola felt it needed a standardized, easily recognizable bottle. They were protective from the beginning, and this was seen in their early advertising: "Demand the Genuine" and "Accept no Substitutes." While the straight-sided bottles were used through 1915, a more unique bottle was needed for the distinctive drink. At this time, bottles were hand blown and not standardized in their sizes. Today's collectors have found a vast amount of bottles to collect. Bottles are classified as amber bottles (ranging in color from brown to honey) and transparent bottles (which include green and blue).

Here's how the Coke bottle evolved over the years:

1894: The Hutchinson bottle was the first bottle used by the Biedenharn Candy Co.

1899-1902: The Hutchinson bottle was the first bottle marked with the Coca-Cola script.

1900-1916: The straight-sided bottle was the first bottle to use the crown cork closure.

1915: The hobble skirt bottle was designed by the Root Glass Co.

1923: The Christmas bottle was the first universal design which was patented Dec. 25, 1923.

1937: The Christmas bottle was standardized in 1948 to hold 6-1/2 oz.

1957: ACL bottle introduced the first applied color label.

1961: The no-return bottle was the first one-way glass bottle. It was later modified to include a twist cap.

1970: The plastic bottle was an experimental bottle tested from 1970-1975.

There were a few different labels used on the original bottles. The following descriptions should help decipher the year of the bottle. Reproduced labels are made of heavier stock and have more uniformed lines in the background.

1. **1903-1908:** Atlanta label, red and blue printing. "Atlanta, GA" lower right border "Trademark registered, Jan 31st, 1892" in tail of "C."

2. **1907-1913:** Blue and black printing, "Asa G. Candler PT" signature on right border, printing below logo reads "Registered Jan'y 1st 1907 No. 13298" and "United States Patent Office."

3. **1913-1917:** Blue and black printing, "Asa G. Candler PT" signature on lower right border, printing below logo reads "Reg. U.S. Pat. Off.," "Copyright 1907, By Coca-Cola Co."

4. **1915-1917:** Blue and black printing, same as #3, except used for 6-1/2 oz. bottle, added border on lower right, "Minimum Volume 6-1/2 oz."

5. **1917-1919:** Blue and black printing, same as #3 but "Chas H. Candler PT" signature on right border and added border as #4 reads, "Contents 6 Fluid Oz."

A design contest for a standardized bottle was awarded at the 1916 Coca-Cola Bottling Convention. The Root Glass Company of Terre Haute, Ind., designed the contour bottle for the Coca-Cola Company.

In November 1915, the new Coca-Cola bottle was born. It was inspired from a line drawing of a cocoa pod added to a light green glass. By 1920, the standardized hobbleskirt bottle was widely used. The patent date of Nov. 16, 1915 was then blown into the glass bottle below the trademark. Coca-Cola finally registered the hobbleskirt bottle in 1960 and it has become as well known as the drink.

Older bottles can be dated fairly easily if you look for the series of manufacturer's numbers on the base or on the bottom of the bottle. For the number 18-30, for example, the first two digits (18) indicate the mold number. The second two digits (30) indicate the year of manufacture.

Currently, Coca-Cola bottlers code the four numbers somewhat differently. The first digit indicates the year; the second, the mold; the third, the manufacturer's symbol; and the fourth digit, the glass plant.

Another possibility for identification is bottle weight. The empty weight for Coca-Cola bottles get lighter each year (see below).

1916-1936: 14.24 oz.

1937-1956: 14.01 oz.

1957-1958: 13.80 oz.

1958-1962: 13.65 oz.

1966-present: 13.26 oz.

Item	Value
1894-1975: Chronology of the glass package for Coca-Cola	
1894, Biedenharn Candy Company	$250.00
1905, Biedenharn bottle	$280.00
1905, Biedenharn candy	$220.00
1902, Hutchinson bottle	$2,000.00

1894, Biedenharn Candy Company—$250

1894-1975: Chronology of the glass package for Coca-Cola

1905, Biedenharn candy—$220

1902, Hutchinson bottle—$2,000

1905, Biedenharn bottle—$280

Syrup Bottles

Syrup bottles were given to drugstores for storing syrup to be mixed with seltzer. In addition to these bottles, syrup was also delivered in barrels.

Item	Value	Item	Value
1910, Coca-Cola syrup bottle, red script	$650.00	1923, Christmas display bottle	$350.00
1920, Coca-Cola syrup bottle, rectangular etched frame	$600.00	1930, Syrup jug	$125.00
1920, Drink Coca-Cola syrup bottle	$500.00	1930, Syrup can	$400.00
1920, Syrup bottle, wreath frame, metal top	$500.00	1961, Hutchinson commemorative	$375.00
1920, Drink Coca-Cola syrup bottle	$400.00	1971, Root commemorative bottle with box	$500.00
		1974, Experimental plastic bottle	$45.00

1910, Coca-Cola syrup bottle, red script—$650

1920, Coca-Cola syrup bottle, rectangular etched frame—$600

1920, Drink Coca-Cola syrup bottle—$500

1920, Drink Coca-Cola syrup bottle—$400

1920, Syrup bottle, wreath frame, metal top—$500

1923, Christmas display bottle—$350

1974, Experimental plastic bottle—$45

1961, Hutchinson commemorative—$375

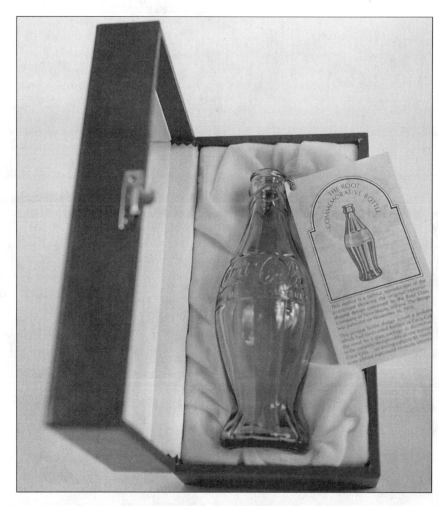

1971, Root commemorative bottle with box—$500

1930, Syrup jug—$125

1930, Syrup can—$400

Seltzer Bottles

Item	Value
Bradford, PA (blue)	$275.00
Billings, MT	$400.00

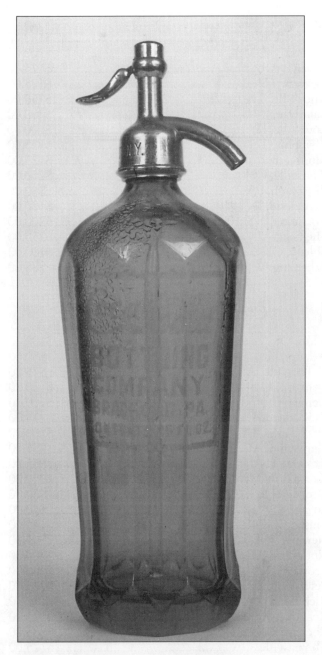

Seltzer bottle, Bradford, PA (blue)—$275

Seltzer bottle, Billings, MT—$400

Amber Bottles (1905-1916)

Item	Value
Cincinnati, OH	$125.00
Clarksdale, MS	$175.00
Cleveland, OH	$125.00
Cumberland, MD	$175.00
Dalton, GA	$325.00
Dayton, OH	$150.00
Greenwood, MS	$200.00
Helena, AR	$125.00
Jackson, TN	$125.00
Knoxville, TN	$150.00
Lafayette, IN	$300.00
Louisville, KY	$100.00
Memphis, TN	$125.00
Murfreesboro, TN	$125.00
Painsville, OH	$250.00
Pittsburgh, PA	$80.00
Richmond, IN 1910	$100.00
Rochester, NY, 10 oz.	$200.00
Sheffield, AL	$150.00
Toledo, OH	$100.00
Wheeling, WV	$85.00

Clear Bottles (1905-1916)

Item	Value
Altus, OK	$100.00
Atlanta, GA	$50.00
Collinsville, AL	$75.00
Denver, CO 8-1/2"	$100.00
Denver, CO 7-1/4"	$100.00
DeRidder, LA	$225.00
Des Moines, IA	$100.00
Huntsville, AL	$75.00
Jackson, TN	$65.00
Kalamazoo, MI	$100.00
Litchfield, IL	$60.00
Logan, WV	$50.00
Muskogee, OK	$145.00
Newbern, NC	$45.00
Notasulga, AL	$200.00
Peoria, IL	$200.00
Petersburg, IL	$225.00
Richmond, VA	$125.00
Roanoke, AL	$75.00
Rochester, NY	$285.00
Thomasville, GA	$125.00

Amber bottle, Greenwood, MS—$200

Calendars

The first Coca-Cola calendar was issued in 1891. The first 10 years displayed wholesome and pretty, yet anonymous, girls. As the company grew, they were able to engage the desirable actress Hilda Clark and the celebrated Metropolitan Opera star, Lillian Nordica, as models. After 1920, most calendars were released once again with unnamed models.

Many calendars were printed in two versions, one with the model holding a Coca-Cola glass—the other, a Coca-Cola bottle. Since these calendars were distributed by bottlers, there are more calendars displaying bottles than glasses.

It is very difficult to find a calendar complete with pad and all calendar pages intact. Without pad or pages, calendars cannot be considered in mint condition. They are still very beautiful and valuable.

Item	Value
1891, First Coca-Cola calendar, 6-1/2" x 9", printed by Calvert Lithography Co., of Atlanta	$15,000.00
1897, First calendar with free coupon offering a Coca-Cola	$9,000.00
1898, Calendar illustration without the pad	$2,000.00
1899, Sold Everywhere 5c	$10,000.00
1901, 7-3/8" x 13"	$7,500.00

Item	Value
1901, 7-5/8" x 11"	$10,000.00
1902, Photograph of Hilda Clark, printing done by Wolf and Company, Philadelphia, ©1900 by Morrison of Chicago	$6,000.00

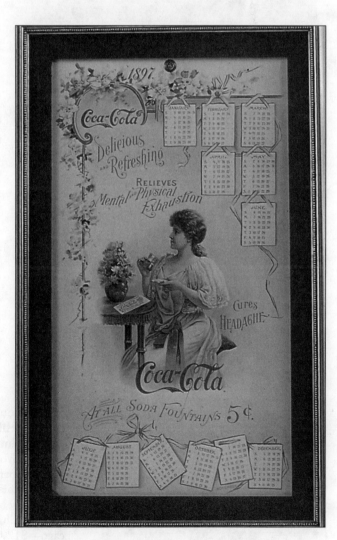

1891, First Coca-Cola calendar, 6-1/2" x 9", printed by Calvert Lithography Co., of Atlanta—$15,000

1897, First calendar with free coupon offering a Coca-Cola—$9,000

1898, Calendar illustration without the pad—
$2,000

1901, 7-3/8" x 13"—$7,500

1899, Sold Everywhere 5c—$10,000

1902, Photograph of Hilda Clark, printing done by Wolf and Company, Philadelphia, ©1900 by Morrison of Chicago—$12,000

Item	Value	Item	Value
1903, This calendar displays the same glassholder used in the 1902 issue	$8,500.00	1915	$4,000.00
1904, This calendar exists with two versions, instead of the glass on the table, there is a bottle	$4,500.00	1916, 1917 World War I girl	$2,050.00
1906, 7-3/4" x 14-1/4"	$6,500.00	1917, Issued with glass or bottle	$2,600.00
1907, 7" x 14"	$7,500.00	1918	$5,000.00
1908, Good to the last drop (Maxwell House later trademarked this slogan for use with its products)	$5,500.00	1919, 1916 Knitting girl	$4,000.00
1909, Same photograph as the 1904 calendar	$6,000.00	1919, 6-1/4" x 10-1/2", Marion Davies	$4,500.00
1910	$6,500.00	1920	$2,350.00
1911	$6,000.00	1921	$2,100.00
1912, First calendar to use two models. 16" x 22"	$5,000.00	1922, Autumn girl	$1,750.00
1913	$4,000.00	1923	$975.00
1914, Betty is one of the most popular Coca-Cola girls	$1,800.00	1924	$1,300.00
		1925	$1,150.00
		1927	$1,100.00
		1926	$1,500.00
		1928	$1,200.00

1903, This calendar displays the same glassholder used in the 1902 issue—$8,500

1906, 7-3/4" x 14-1/4"—$6,500

1904, This calendar exists with two versions, instead of the glass on the table, there is a bottle—$4,500

1909, Same photograph as the 1904 calendar—$6,000

1907, 7" x 14"—$7,500

1908, Good to the last drop (Maxwell House later trademarked this slogan for use with its products)—$5,500

1910—$6,500

1911—$6,000

1914, Betty is one of
the most popular Coca-
Cola girls—$1,800

1912, First calendar to use two models.
16" x 22"—$5,000

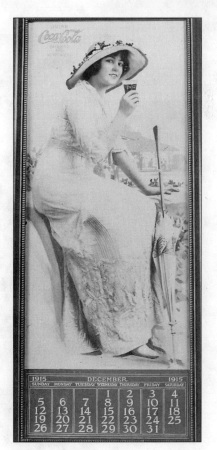

1915—$4,000

1916, 1917
World War I
girl—$2,050

1918—$5,000

1917, Issued with glass
or bottle—$2,600

1919, 1916
Knitting girl—
$4,000

1919, 6-1/4" x
10-1/2", Marion
Davies—$4,500

1921—$2,100

1920—$2,350

1922, Autumn girl—$1,750

1923—$975

1925—$1,150

1924—$1,300

1927—$1,100

Calendars

1926—$1,500

1929—$1,300

1928—$1,200

1930, Bathing beauty—$1,150

1931, Farm boy with dog by Norman Rockwell, a.k.a., "Tom Sawyer"—$975

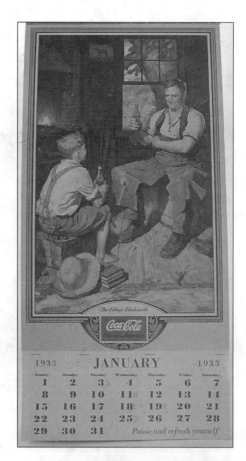

1933, Village blacksmith by Frederic Stanley—$825

1932, Huckleberry Finn by Norman Rockwell—$800

1934, Norman Rockwell—$800

1935, Norman
Rockwell—$775

1937, N.C. Wyeth—$725

1936, Artist
N.C Wyeth,
N.C Wyeth—
$875

1938, by Bradshaw Crandell—$625

Item	Value
1929	$1,300.00
1930, Bathing beauty	$1,150.00
1931, Farm boy with dog by Norman Rockwell, a.k.a., "Tom Sawyer"	$975.00
1932, Huckleberry Finn by Norman Rockwell	$800.00
1933, Village blacksmith by Frederic Stanley	$825.00
1934, Norman Rockwell	$800.00
1935, Norman Rockwell	$775.00
1936, N.C Wyeth	$875.00
1937, N.C. Wyeth	$725.00
1938, Created by Bradshaw Crandall	$625.00
1939, Glass in this calendar is unmarked	$550.00
1940, The Pause That Refreshes	$550.00
1941, Thirst Knows No Season	$425.00
1942, Thirst Knows No Season	$380.00
1943, Calendar honoring the US	$450.00
1963, Reference calendar	$15.00
1964, Reference calendar	$15.00
1965, Reference calendar	$15.00
1966, Reference calendar	$15.00
1967, Reference calendar	$10.00
1968, Reference calendar	$10.00
1969, Reference calendar	$5.00
1970, Reference calendar	$5.00
1972	$12.50
1973	$12.50

1972—$12.50

1939, Glass in this calendar is unmarked—$550

1973—$12.50

Cars & Trucks

The Metalcraft Company developed a delightful and sturdy toy truck that was used by the Coca-Cola Company. The truck came in four versions: metal wheels; rubber wheels; rubber wheels and working headlights; and, probably the most rare, a truck with a much longer hood.

The Smith-Miller Company was next in line to produce trucks for Coca-Cola in the 1940s and 1950s. These trucks were made of wood or wood with metal cabs. Most of these Coca-Cola toy trucks were painted in the familiar red.

The yellow metal trucks from the Buddy L Company are the most easily attainable. These trucks, produced in the 1950s and 1960s and continuing through the 1970s and 1980s, are abundant and readily accessible to collectors.

The Marx Company made several tin and plastic trucks that were used to advertise Coca-Cola. Matchbox trucks are common and available still in their original box. The "cars and trucks" category is a popular and satisfying one for collectors. It should be noted that any item is more valuable when collected with the original box or container.

Item	Value
1930, Metalcraft truck, metal wheels	$825.00
1930, Metalcraft truck, 11", rubber wheels	$1,250.00
1930, Metalcraft truck	$900.00
1930, Metalcraft truck, rubber wheels and working headlights	$1,000.00
1945, Sprite boy, red & yellow	$550.00
1945, Sprite boy, yellow with red, white & blue	$775.00
1950, Coke truck	$600.00
1950, Open truck	$450.00
1950, Car	$420.00
1950, VW bus, friction motion	$275.00
1950, VW van	$325.00
1950s, Truck, 3"	$330.00
1950s, Yellow and red tin, 4-1/4"	$175.00
1950s, Pull-out bottles, 8-1/2"	$800.00
1950s, Delivery truck	$85.00
1950s, Marx	$1,200.00
1950s, Enclosed truck	$400.00
1950s, Ford station wagon 5"	$350.00
1950s, Marx truck	$400.00
1950s, Marx truck, plastic	$450.00

Item	Value
1956, Drink Coca-Cola Refreshed	$625.00
1958, Early Matchbook truck, 2-1/4"	$125.00
1958, Early Matchbook truck, with black wheels, 2-1/4"	$75.00
1960, Buddy L truck	$595.00
1960s, Delivery truck	$125.00
1960s, Tin, friction, Japan	$1,300.00
1960s, Buddy L	$325.00
1960s, Pickup, 8" long	$65.00
1960s, Things Go Better With Coke 4-1/2"	$50.00
1960s, Truck 2-3/4"	$50.00
1970s, Buddy L hand truck, 9"	$75.00
1979, Delivery Truck with Coke cases	$60.00
1979, Buddy L Delivery Truck with Coke cases	$50.00
1960s, Cast iron, fishtail-shaped	$140.00
1970s, Plastic	$50.00
1970s, Tin, Japan	$225.00
1970, Flatbed 1-1/2"	$50.00
1971, Roadster model	$40.00
1972, Coke can car	$35.00
1972, Semi truck	$325.00
1973, Truck	$80.00
1974, Eight-wheeler truck	$50.00
1974, Modern logo truck	$35.00
1974, Zip a Long, Hong Kong	$50.00
1975, Bus, double-decker	$35.00

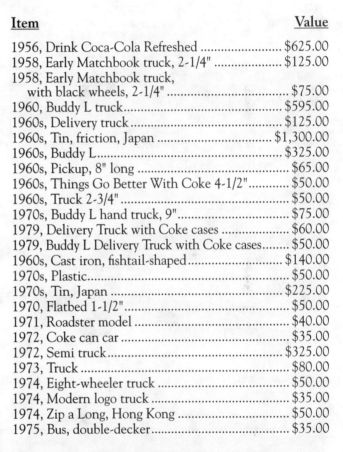

1930, Metalcraft truck, metal wheels—$825

1945, Sprite boy, red & yellow—$550

1945, Sprite boy, yellow with red, white & blue—$775

1950, VW van—$325

1950, Open truck—$450

1950s, Truck, 3"—$330

1950, Car—$420

1950s, Yellow and red tin, 4-1/4"—$175

1950, VW bus, friction motion—$275

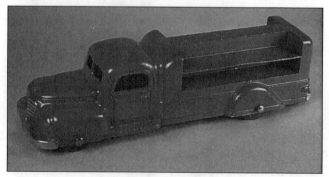

1950s, Marx—$1,200

Cars & Trucks

1950s, Pull-out bottles, 8-1/2"—$800

1960, Buddy L truck—$595

1950s, Delivery truck—$85

1956, Drink Coca-Cola Refreshed—$625

1960s, Delivery truck—$125

1958, Early Matchbook truck, 2-1/4"—$125

1960s, Tin, friction, Japan—$1,300

Cars & Trucks

1960s, Buddy L—$325

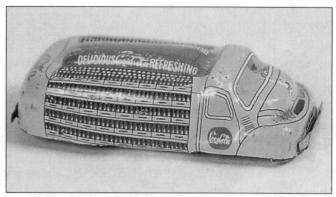

1970s, Tin, Japan—$225

1960s, Cast iron, fishtail-shaped—$140

1972, Coke can car—$35

1970s, Plastic—$50

23. 1972, Semi truck—$325

1974, Zip a Long, Hong Kong—
$50

1973, Truck—$80

1974, Eight-wheeler truck—$50

1975, Bus, double-decker—$35

Cartons, Cases & Coolers

The Coca-Cola Company made it even more convenient when it introduced the six-bottle carton in 1920. An early example of a six-bottle carrier was a wooden box with a rope handle. Another example of a six-bottle carrier was a corrugated printed box that was returnable along with the six bottles. The first coolers used for keeping bottles cold were simple wooden cases with the familiar trademark stenciled on the outside.

Originally, when Coca-Cola bottles were given to retailers to sell, these shopkeepers had the responsibility to keep the bottles cold. They placed them in the refrigerators along with milk, eggs and cheese. However, if they needed the room for the other products that could spoil, the Coca-Cola was then not refrigerated. Coca-Cola felt it was very important to keep a chill on its product for proper taste and carbonation. Therefore, the company decided to take steps to ensure that it was kept cold.

The first coolers, issued by Coca-Cola, were containers or tubs that simply held ice. Bottles would be placed to chill in these tubs. This also made it possible to strategically display Coca-Cola rather have it be hidden, usually in back, of the refrigerators. The next progression for this case or tub was to place it on legs and add some type of lid, either hinged or sliding. To better insulate the ice and keep it from melting so quickly, sheet metal was attached to the sides of the container.

Always wanting uniformity, Coca-Cola developed a prototype cooler by Glascock Brothers Manufacturing Company of Muncie, Ind. The new cooler was introduced at the 1929 Coca-Cola bottlers convention. The salesman's sample coolers were miniatures used to demonstrate the exciting new features. The Glascock Coolers were later replaced in 1935 when coin-operated vending machines made the cold taste of pop convenient for everyone. In the mid-1930s, Westinghouse developed the first coin-operated vending machine.

Item	Value
1917, Shipping case	$250.00
1924, Bottle carrier	$275.00
1929, Glascock, single case, junior size	$1,800.00
1929, Glascock, double case, full size	$1,200.00
1930, Glascock, electric cooler	$2,600.00
1933, 6-bottle holder	$100.00
1934, Bottle ice cooler, held block ice to cool bottles	$950.00
1935, July 4th wrapper	$250.00
1937, 6-bottle holder	$100.00

Item	Value
1939, Take-home carton	$175.00
1939, Westinghouse 24" x 30" x 34"	$550.00
1940s, Westinghouse 6-case electric	$650.00
1940s, Westinghouse 3-case, junior electric	$575.00
1940, Take-home carton	$150.00
1940, Take-home carton	$175.00
1940, Car window holder	$35.00
1950, Car bottle holder	$45.00
1950s, 2-bottle holder for shopping cart	$35.00

1917, Shipping case—$250

1924, Bottle carrier—$275

1933, 6-bottle holder—$100

1934, Bottle ice cooler, held block ice to cool bottles—$950

1935, July 4th wrapper—$250

Cartons, Cases & Coolers

1937, 6-bottle holder—$100

1940, Take-home carton—$150

1940, Take-home carton—$175

1939, Take-home carton—$175

Cartons, Cases & Coolers

1940, Car window holder—$35

1950s, 2-bottle holder for shopping cart—$35

1950, Car bottle holder—$45

Salesman's samples

Item	Value
1929, Salesman's sample cooler	$5,500.00
1934, Salesman's sample cooler	$3,200.00
1934, Salesman's sample cooler	$3,400.00

1934, Salesman's sample cooler—$3,200

1929, Salesman's sample cooler—$5,500

1934, Salesman's sample cooler—$3,400

Chewing Gum

While most people associate the familiar Coca-Cola trademark with the popular soda, the logo has also been used to represent other items. In 1908, the Franklin Manufacturing Company of Richmond, Va., produced a chicle that "aids digestion and gives comfort after a hearty meal." Coca-Cola Pepsin Gum was introduced in a catalog by Schaack & Sons of Chicago. Twenty packages, 5 cents each, sold wholesale for 60 cents. My father discovered the one-of-a-kind 1902 cylindrical gum dispenser from a gum dispenser collector. When my father later sold it to the Schmidt Museum, this one-of-a-kind collectible brought top dollar.

Another exciting collectible is a glass Coca-Cola Chewing Gum roulette wheel. This wheel was displayed for many years on a drugstore counter in a small South Carolina town. It is the size of a dinner plate and weighs three or four pounds. A marble rolls around the interior circumference of the wheel and drops into one of the numbered slots in the center. In 1980, an antique store merchant from South Carolina wrote after reading my monthly column. He had acquired this roulette piece 20 years earlier from the estate of a woman who had once owned the above mentioned drugstore. He kept the roulette wheel on the counter after he bought the store. This roulette wheel has the second highest value of any chewing gum-related item.

Item	Value
1902, Coca-Cola gum	$2,500.00
1902, Cylindrical gum	$3,000.00
1902, Cylindrical gum dispenser	$12,000.00
1904, Ad in *Everybody's* magazine	$150.00
1906, Gum package wrapper, spearmint	$650.00
1906, Gum package wrapper, peppermint	$650.00
1904, Bookmark, "The Gum That's Pure Contains The Tonic Properties of Coca-Cola and Pure Pepsin"	$2,000.00

Item	Value
1906, Shipping case	$400.00
1908, Glass roulette wheel	$8,300.00
1910, Coca-Cola gum fan, front (front of fan shows the Franklin Caro Manufacturing Company, Richmond, Va.)	$2,000.00
1910, Coca-Cola fan, back	
1913, Gum dispenser box	$2,500.00
1913, Gum display shipping box	$1,500.00
1915, Apothecary jars, chewing gum	$900.00
1915, Apothecary jars, pepsin gum	$900.00

1902, Coca-Cola gum—$2,500

1902, Cylindrical gum—$3,000

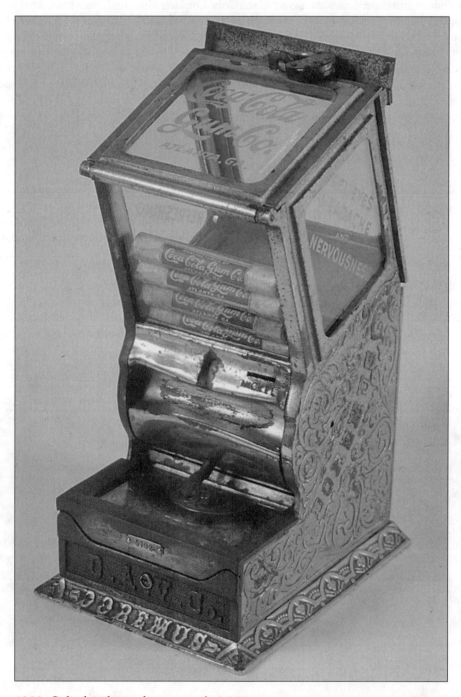

1902, Cylindrical gum dispenser—$12,000

1904, Ad in *Everybody's* magazine—$150

1906, Gum package wrapper, spearmint—$650

1906, Gum package wrapper, peppermint—$650

1904, Bookmark, "The Gum That's Pure Contains The Tonic Properties of Coca-Cola and Pure Pepsin"—$2,000

1906, Shipping case—$400

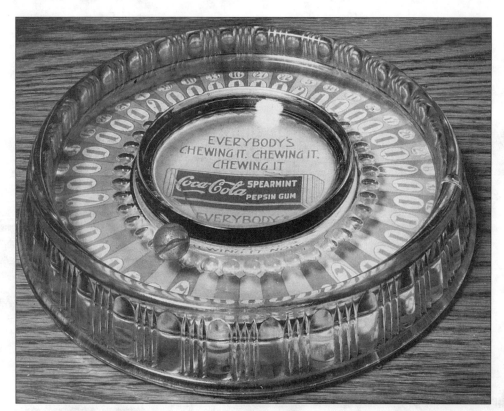

1908, Glass roulette
wheel—$8,300

1910, Coca-Cola fan, back

1910, Coca-Cola gum fan, front (front of fan
shows the Franklin Caro Manufacturing Company, Richmond, Va.)—$2,000

1913, Gum dispenser box—$2,500

1913, Gum display shipping box—$1,500

1915, Apothecary jars, chewing gum—$900

1915, Apothecary jars, pepsin gum—$900

Clocks

Baird Clock Company produced the first clock used to promote Coca-Cola. Soda fountains that sold more than 100 gallons of syrup a year were able to obtain a clock. The advertisement was embossed on the circular plaster-of-Paris frame. Two types of Baird Clocks are known to exist—the figure eight and gallery. Baird moved his plant to Chicago in 1896. These clocks gained a new look complete with wooden case and the advertising slogan embossed with tin.

The Ingraham clocks used from 1903 to 1907 were both the schoolhouse clock and the regulator. They both had eight-day movements and were key wound. The company later standardized its advertising message and promoted "Drink Coca-Cola" on all clocks. The Gilbert Clocks from the 1920s have become easier to obtain. They are also easier to identify. There is a sticker on the back which states, "The Wm. L. Gilbert Clock Co., Winsted, Conn." They were well made and dependable.

Electric clocks made their appearance in the early 1930s with neon enhancements following in the 1940s. Collectors love collectibles that light up, and the clocks in the 1950s and 1960s don't disappoint. Collectors love finding a clock. It becomes both easy to display and, if it works, a useful collectible.

Item	Value
1892, Baird clock	$6,750.00
1893, Baird clock	$5,250.00
1907, Desk clock, embossed bottles	$2,000.00
1907, Desk clock	$1,700.00
1910, Drink Coca-Cola	$3,900.00
1910, Dome clock	$1,500.00
1915, Wall clock	$1,300.00
1920, Pocket watch	$1,650.00
1930s, Octagonal neon silhouette clock, 18"	$2,100.00
1930s, Selecto Clock 16" x 16"	$650.00
1930s, Seth Thomas white frame clock, 18"	$700.00
1930, Silhouette clock with metal frame, 18" diameter	$775.00
1939, Wood framed Selecto clock, 16" x 16"	$500.00
1950s, Round silver tin clock	$200.00
1950s, Lighted clock with silhouette red center with green border	$450.00
1950s, Round brown tin clock	$175.00
1950, Dome clock, two bottles	$925.00
1960s, Lighted fishtail clock	$250.00
1972, Reissue clock	$65.00
1974, Reissue Betty clock	$65.00

1892, Baird clock—$6,750

1893, Baird clock—$5,250

1907, Desk clock—$1,700

1910, Drink Coca-Cola—$3,900

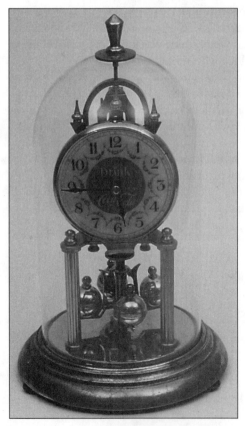

1907, Desk clock, embossed bottles—$2,000

1910, Dome
clock—$1,500

1915, Wall clock—$1,300

1920, Pocket watch—$1,650

1950, Dome clock, two bottles—$925

1974, Reissue Betty clock—$65

1972, Reissue clock —$65

Coupons

Item	Value	Item	Value
1900, Hilda Clark, front	$700.00	1920, Coupon book	$20.00
1900, Hilda Clark, back	$700.00	1920, Individual coupon	$15.00
1900, The Coca-Cola girl, 1-1/2" x 3-3/8"	$290.00	1927, Soda jerk	$75.00
1903, Purple and green, 1-5/8" x 3-3/8"	$350.00	1928, Golfer	$35.00
1904, Lillian Russell	$400.00	1929, Refresh Yourself	$65.00
1904, Delicious and Refreshing	$275.00	1939, Take Home a Carton	$15.00
1905, Lillian Nordica, 6-1/2" x 9-3/4"	$250.00	1940-50s, Coca-Cola coupon	$20.00
1908, Purple, 1-5/8" x 3-3/8"	$200.00	1940-50s, Free, Six Bottles	$20.00

1900, Hilda Clark, front—$700

1903, Purple and green, 1-5/8" x 3-3/8"—$350

1900, Hilda Clark, back—$700

1900, The Coca-Cola girl, 1-1/2" x 3-3/8"—$290

1904, Lillian Russell—$400

1904, Delicious and Refreshing—$275

1905, Lillian Nordica, 6-1/2" x 9-3/4"—
$250

1920, Individual coupon—$15

1927, Soda jerk—$75

1908, Purple, 1-5/8" x 3-3/8"—$200

1928, Golfer—$35

1940-50s, Coca-Cola coupon—$20

1929, Refresh Yourself—$65

1939, Take Home a Carton—$15

1940-50s, Free, Six Bottles—$20

Famous People and Coca-Cola

A few years before the discovery of Coca-Cola, the Metropolitan Opera opened its doors for the first time. While Coca-Cola was growing, an opera house joined the soda fountain in every town as a part of everyday life around the country. So it seemed natural that Lillian Nordica, a famous Metropolitan Opera star, should be the first to support Coca-Cola. This endorsement from stars like Nordica and Hilda Clark helped make Coca-Cola synonymous with the beautiful glamorous lifestyles of the late 1900s.

As the century changed, so did the world. We became less formal and more fun. Young and charming men and women portrayed the pleasures of life while sipping a glass or a bottle of Coca-Cola. Whether they were golfing, playing tennis, skating or boating, they portrayed their life of good taste and leisure, a lifestyle synonymous with Coca-Cola. As the movie business grew into Hollywood, movie stars became the spokespeople for their favorite drink. They were featured on advertisements, signs and cutouts.

The following is a list of famous celebrities who lent their names and faces to help promote the world's most famous drink: Adrienne Ames, Richard Arlen, Lionel Barrymore, Wallace Beery, Tony Bennett, Edgar Bergen, Joan Blondell, Billie Burke, Sue Carol, Hilda Clark, Claudette Colbert, June Collyer, Jackie Cooper, Joan Crawford, George Cukor, Marion Davies, Francis Dee, Morton Downey, Marie Dressler, Madge Evans, Percy Faith, Eddie Fisher, Clark Gable, Cary Grant, Lionel Hampton, Jean Harlow, Benita Hume, Spike Jones, Kay Kayser, Andre Kostelanetz, Lola Lane, Mario Lanza, Laura La Plante, Carol Lombard, Edmund Lowe, Frederic March, The McGuire Sisters, Graham McNamee, Ricki Nelson, Ray Noble, Lillian Nordica, Maureen O'Sullivan, Gene Raymond, Grantland Rice, Genevieve Tobin, Lupe Velez, Johnny Weissmuller, Pearl White, Bill Williams and Loretta Young.

Cutouts

Item	Value	Item	Value
(Depending on condition) 1932—Jean Harlow, Joan Blondell, Lupe Velez, Sue Carol; 1933—Carole Lombard & Phillip Holmes, Frederic March & Claudette Colbert, Richard Arlen & Adrienne Ames; 1934—Wallace Beery & Jackie Cooper .....$4,000-$5,000 each		1954, Eddie Fisher, 5" .... $2,000.00 1954, Eddie Fisher, 19" $1,200.00	

Photos

Item	Value	Item	Value
1932, Sue Carol $100.00		1933, Maureen O'Sullivan.....................................$100.00	
1932, Jean Harlow & Clark Gable......................$250.00		1933, Joan Crawford $100.00	
1932, Jean Harlow $200.00		1950, Eddie Fisher..$35.00	
1933, Johnny Weissmuller & Maureen O'Sullivan $325.00			

Fans

These fans were given to stores and distributed to customers.

Item	Value
1911, Keep Cool, Drink Coca-Cola	$200.00
1920s, Save With Ice	$100.00
1930s, Drink Coca-Cola	$85.00
1950s, Quality Carries On	$50.00
1950, Drink Coca-Cola	$60.00
1960s, Drive With Care	$85.00
1960s, Drink Coca-Cola	$40.00

1920s, Save With Ice—$100

1911, Keep Cool, Drink Coca-Cola—
$200

1930s, Drink Coca-Cola—$85

1960s, Drink Coca-Cola—$40

1950s, Quality Carries On—$50

1950, Drink Coca-Cola—$60

1960s, Drive With Care—$85

Festoons

Item	Value	Item	Value
1912, Balloons	$5,500.00	1950s, Antique cars	$650.00
1914, Follow The Crowd	$6,500.00	1950, Antique cars	$650.00
1922, Autumn leaves	$1,250.00	1950, Square dance	$650.00
1926, Fans	$4,800.00	1950, State tree	$550.00
1926, Chinese lanterns	$6,000.00	1951, Coca-Cola girls	$900.00
1927, Coca-Cola girls	$4,000.00	1951, Girls' heads	$1,200.00
1928, Coca-Cola girls	$5,000.00	1958, Coca-Cola girls	$650.00
1930s, Icicles	$900.00	1951, Cornflower	$3,500.00
1930s, Swans	$1,000.00	1951, Hollyhock	$2,500.00
1931, Poinsettia	$2,200.00	1951, Morning glory	$4,000.00
1939, Petunia	$1,300.00	1951, Verbena	$2,500.00

Festoon: 1928, Coca-Cola girls—$5,000

Glass Items & Dishes

Item	Value
1895, Syrup dispenser	$5,000.00
1900, Ceramic change receiver	$5,000.00
1901, Glass change receiver	$5,000.00
1907, Glass change receiver, Charles Lippincott & Company, Philadelphia	$1,500.00
1920, Milk glass light fixture (beautiful milk glass light fixture was available from the Progress Fixture Company, New York. "Property of the Coca-Cola Company" marked on top band)	$2,000.00
1920, Milk glass shade	$1,200.00
1920, Leaded glass bottle, 36" high	$9,500.00

Item	Value
1920, Snack bowl	$400.00
1928, Leaded glass globe	$8,000.00
1930, China plate	$425.00
1930s, Aluminum pretzel dish	$225.00
1950, Lenox china plate	$475.00
1967, World dish (shows where Coca-Cola is sold around the world)	$100.00
1967, World dish	$100.00
1969, Swedish glass plate	$100.00

1895, Syrup dispenser—$5,000

1900, Ceramic change receiver—$5,000

1901, Glass change receiver—$5,000

1907, Glass change receiver,
Charles Lippincott & Company,
Philadelphia—$1,500

1920, Milk glass light fixture (beautiful milk glass light fixture was available from the Progress Fixture Company, New York. "Property of the Coca-Cola Company" marked on top band)—$2,000

1920, Leaded glass bottle, 36" high—$9,500

1920, Milk glass shade—$1,200

Glass Items & Dishes

1920, Snack bowl—$400

1930, China plate—$425

1930s, Aluminum pretzel dish—$225

1928, Leaded glass globe—$8,000

1950, Lenox china plate—$475

1967, World dish (shows where Coca-Cola is sold around the world.)—$100

1967, World dish—$100

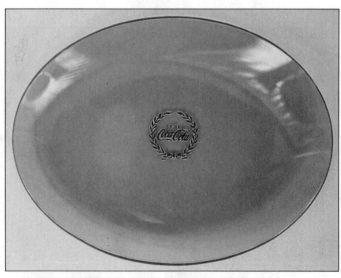

1969, Swedish glass plate—$100

Glasses

Like the famous contour bottles, Coca-Cola wanted an instantly recognizable glass for the famous drink. There were only a few types of Coca-Cola glasses used in the early years, which makes them even more collectible. Within each category are several distinctions including different words: "Drink," "Bottle," "Enjoy," "5c" and the trademark, "Coca-Cola."

In 1900, Coca-Cola began by using a "graduated" Coke glass. The company took a normal straight-sided glass, a soda water glass and added the famous Coca-Cola script trademark. Almost an inch from the bottom was the "graduated" line showing how much syrup was to put into the glass. Before automation, these glasses were filled with syrup to the line and then ice and carbonated water added to the top of the glass. This glass was important to Coca-Cola for consistency of product. Just the right amount of syrup made the drink what it is today. Coca-Cola designed a special metal holder for the straight-sided glasses.

In 1905, the company introduced the "bell" or "flare" glass. This glass was smaller at the bottom and gradually flared as it got to the top. The "modified flare" was introduced in 1923. This flare glass had a unique turned edge at the rim. By 1926, with 4 million modified flare glasses in use, Coca-Cola made its last modification. In 1929, the final change, an even more pronounced edge was given to the glass. The glass also had a distinct bulge about half an inch from the top of the glass.

In 1955, testing began for a larger glass, and the new 12 oz. glass became a huge success. By 1961, a 16 oz. glass was introduced to accommodate Coke floats.

Item	Value
1912, Coca-Cola, 5c, flare (the reproduction of this glass has an "F" on the bottom inside of a sort of triangle)	$1,000.00
1914, Drink Coca-Cola, flare	$450.00
1927, Modified flare	$125.00
1930, Pewter	$350.00
1900s, Silver glass holder, Coca-Cola logo (the reproduction of this item has the word "Drink" above the logo, the original does not have the word "Drink" above the scripted "Coca-Cola")	$1,500.00

1912, Coca-Cola, 5c, flare (the reproduction of this glass has an "F" on the bottom inside of a sort of triangle)—$1,000

1914, Drink Coca-Cola, flare—$450

1927, Modified flare—$125

1930, Pewter—$350

1900s, Silver glass holder, Coca-Cola logo (the reproduction of this item has the word "Drink" above the logo, the original does not have the word "Drink" above the scripted "Coca-Cola")—$1,500

Magazine and Newspaper Advertising

Early advertising showed elaborately dressed people drinking Coca-Cola. The slogans always emphasized the popular Coca-Cola trademark. Advertisements for Coca-Cola appeared frequently in these publications: *The Housekeeper, Women's Home Companion, Ladies Home Journal, Redbook, Better Homes and Gardens, McCall's, Sports Illustrated, National Geographic, Motor Trend, Car Craft, Sports Car Graphics, Hot Rod, Boys Life, American Girl, Seventeen, Saturday Evening Post, Success, Literary Digest, Life, Delineator, Sunset, Pictorial Review and Farm and Home.* Two color ads appeared on both the front and back covers of these publications: *The Housewife, The Household* and *Popular People's Monthly.*

The first newspaper advertisements were most often placed by individual bottlers.

In 1886, *The Daily Journal* ran the first ad for Coca-Cola, which read as follows, "Coca-Cola, Delicious, Refreshing, Exhilarating, Invigorating, The New and popular Soda Fountain Drink, containing the properties of the wonderful Cocoa plant and the famous cola nuts. For sale by Willis Venable and Nunally & Rawson." in 1906, the D'Arcy agency implemented standardized advertising copy. Coca-Cola made many appeals to their distributors for uniformity. In 1926, just over one-half of all bottlers were using company prepared advertisements.

In 1939, Coca-Cola offered their bottlers a cooperative advertising program. Based on per capita consumption within their territory, the company assumed from 50 to 80 percent of all advertising costs. They also provided art for ads that bottlers could place in their local newspapers. Because the company provided adequate advertising, this lessened the amount of individually created advertisements.

Magazine and newspaper advertisements are a pictorial representation of the history of both Coca-Cola and the United States. They are readily available and can be found at reasonable prices. A chronological collection of the advertising slogans of Coca-Cola makes for a very nice collection.

Miniatures

Miniatures are small size replicas of larger items. Coca-Cola made miniatures of bottles, glasses, cases, coolers and vending machines. There are also toy manufacturers that made miniatures so children could play at buying, selling and distributing this popular drink.

Item	Value
1920, Embossed bottles and cases	$200.00
1950, Plastic dispenser	$175.00
1950s, Plastic bank	$25.00
1950, Sales aid	$175.00
1950, Music box	$190.00
1950, Dispenser bank, battery operated	$450.00
1950, Dispenser bank, with box	$700.00
1950, Vending machine bank, 5-1/2"	$225.00
1950, Vending machine bank, 2-1/4" x 3"	$125.00
1950, Miniature bottle lighter	$25.00
1960, Plastic dispenser	65.00
1971, Plastic bottles and case	35.00
1971, King and regular size bottles and case	$100.00
1970s, Plastic bottles and case, red case with green bottles	$25.00
1970s, Plastic bottles and case, yellow case with green bottles	$30.00
1970s, Plastic bottles and case, yellow case with gold bottles	$30.00
1973, Miniature 6-pack	$125.00
1973, Miniature 6-pack, gold metal	$6.00

1920, Embossed bottles and cases—$200

1950, Plastic dispenser—$175

1950, Sales aid—$175

1950, Music box—$190

1950, Dispenser bank, battery operated—$450

1950, Miniature bottle lighter—$25

1950, Vending machine bank, 5-1/2"—$225

1950, Vending machine bank, 2-1/4" x 3"—$125

1973, Miniature 6-pack—$125

1973, Miniature 6-pack, gold metal—$6

1950s, Plastic bank—$25

Miscellaneous Items

Item	Value
1910, Door chain and lock	$75.00
1910, Fountain seat	$400.00
1913, Umbrella, straight-sided bottle	$1,500.00
1913, Umbrella, later version, with contour bottle	$900.00
1915, Convention badge, porcelain inlay	$700.00
1920, Door knob, brass or steel	$550.00
1920, Krumkake maker	$900.00
1920, Planter sconce, cardboard 9" x 13"	$475.00
1920, Thimble	$40.00
1920, Salt & pepper	$350.00
1924, Needle case	$150.00
1925, Needlecase: Girl with a glass and a bottle	$100.00
1924, Needlecase: Girl with a glass and a bottle	$95.00
1924, Perfume bottle	$400.00
1926, Magic lantern	$125.00
1930, Door push	$350.00
1930, Driver's hat pin	$200.00
1930, Hatchet, metal head with wooden handle	$450.00
1930, Token	$20.00
1940, Comb	$5.00
1940, First aid kit	$35.00
1940, Pillow	$75.00
1941, Navy sewing kit, WWII	$60.00
1941, Token holder	$75.00
1943, Sugar book	$40.00
1945, Float bottle	$15.00
1950s, Tin pull plate	$300.00
1950, Kit Carson	$85.00
1950, Mileage info, plastic	$1,000.00
1950, Mileage table, 8" diameter	$75.00
1950, License plate	$35.00
1950, Car keys	$35.00
1950, Door push	$200.00
1955, Keychain	$30.00

1910, Fountain seat—$400

1913, Umbrella, straight-sided bottle—$1,500

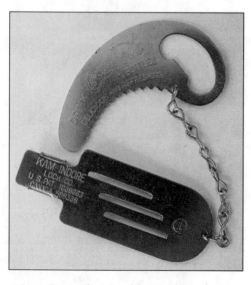

1910, Door chain and lock—$75

1915, Convention badge, porcelain inlay—
$700

1920, Door knob, brass or steel—$550

1920, Krumkake maker—$900

1920, Planter
sconce, card-
board 9" x
13"—$475

1920, Thim-
ble—$40

1920, Salt & pepper—$350

1924, Perfume bottle—$400

1924, Needle case—$150

1926, Magic lantern—$125

1930, Door push—$350

1930, Driver's
hat pin—$200

1940, First aid kit—$35

1930, Token—$20

1930, Hatchet, metal head with wooden handle—$450

Needlecase: 1910, Girl with a glass and a bottle—$100

Needlecase: 1924, Girl with a glass and a bottle—$95

Miscellaneous Items

1940, Pillow—$75

1941, Navy sewing kit, WWII—$60

1940, Comb—$5

1943, Sugar book—$40

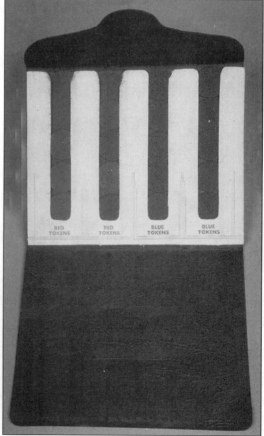

1941, Token holder—$75

Miscellaneous Items

1945, Float bottle—$15

1950s, Tin pull plate—$300

1950, Kit Carson—$85

1950, Mileage info, plastic—$1,000

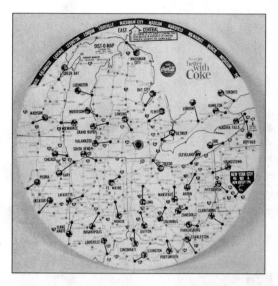

1950, Mileage table, 8" diameter—$75

1950, License plate—$35

1955, Keychain—$30

1950, Car keys—$35

1950, Door push—$200

Miscellaneous Items

Openers

Item	Value
1910, Opener	$90.00
1910, Block print opener	$140.00
1920, Opener	$65.00
1920, Legs opener	$200.00
1920, Boot knife opener	$350.00
1920, Skate key opener	$100.00
1930, Spoon opener	$100.00
1920-30s, "Saber" or "Sword"	$200.00
1928-40, Coca-Cola in bottles	$8.00
1930, Coca-Cola in sterilized bottles	$45.00
1940s, Starr X, wall mounted	$10.00
1940s, Starr X, opener and cap catcher	$15.00
1940, Have a Coke	$5.00
1950, Flat-shaped bottle opener	$50.00
1952, Fiftieth anniversary	$75.00
Drink Coca-Cola	$25.00
1960-80, Beer-type opener	$4.00

1910, Opener—$90

1920, Opener—$65

1920, Boot knife opener—$350

1910, Block print opener—$140

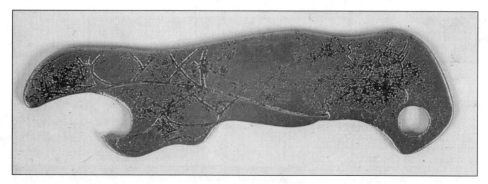

1920, Legs opener—$200

1920, Skate key opener—$100

1920-30s, "Saber" or
"Sword"—$200

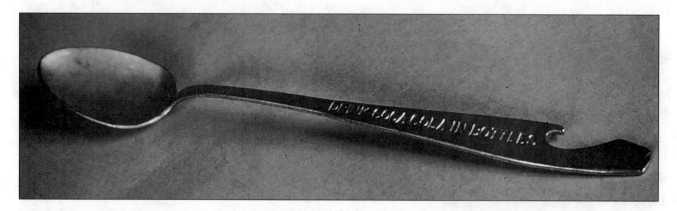

1930, Spoon opener—$100

Openers

1930, Coca-Cola in sterilized bottles—$45

1928-40, Coca-Cola in bottles opener—$8

1940, Have a Coke opener—$5

1940s, Starr X, wall mounted opener—$10

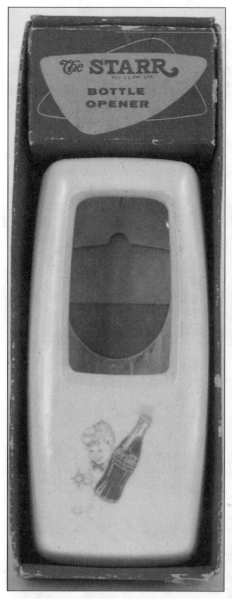

1940s, Starr X, opener and cap
catcher—$15

1950, Flat-shaped bottle opener
—$50

1952, Fiftieth anniversary opener—$75

1960-80, Beer-type opener—$4

Drink Coca-Cola opener—$25

Paper Items

Item	Value
1889, Letterhead, Asa Candler Co.	$200.00
1889, Letterhead	$100.00
1900, Letterhead	$125.00
1901, Celluloid postage stamp holder	$500.00
1903, Hilda Clark celluloid note pad, 2-1/2" x 5"	$700.00
1905, Trade card	$800.00
1905, Note pad, 2-3/4" x 5"	$200.00
1906, Opera program	$600.00
1910, Folding advertising card sent out on a monthly basis, "The Man Across The Way"	$850.00

Item	Value
1910, Folding advertising card, "The Race"	$850.00
1910, Folding advertising card, "The Attractive Teacher"	$850.00
1910, Folding advertising card, "The Wooden Horse"	$850.00
1929, Miniature ad	$100.00
1931, Souvenir money, Confederate $100 bill	$75.00
1932, Bottle bags	$15.00
1941, Score pad	$35.00
1948, Plant tour gift	$20.00
1950, Pocket secretary (given to bottling company management within, pen inside)	$25.00

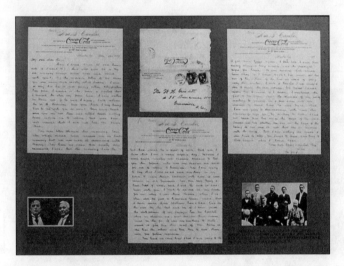

17-2. 1889, Letterhead—$200

17-3. 1900, Letterhead—$125

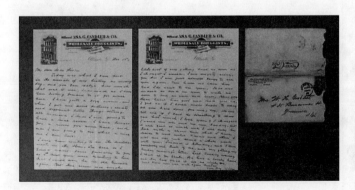

1889, Letterhead, Asa Candler Co.—$200

1903, Hilda Clark celluloid note pad, 2-1/2" x 5"—$700

1905, Trade card, unfolded—$800

1905, Trade card, folded

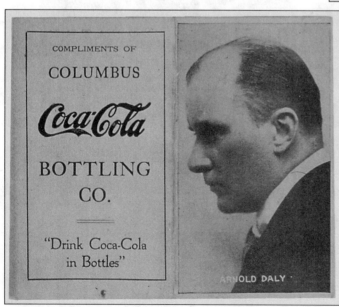

1906, Opera program—$600

Paper Items

1910, Folding advertising card sent out monthly—$850

1910, Folding advertising card, "The Race"—$850

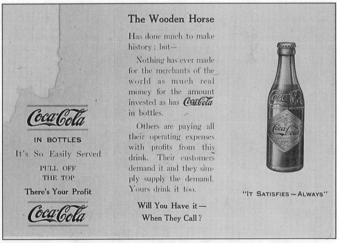

1910, Folding advertising card, "The Wooden Horse"—$850

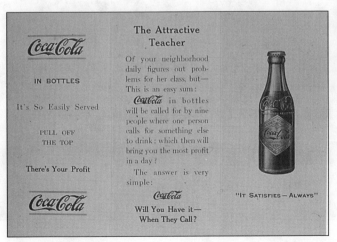

1910, Folding advertising card, "The Attractive Teacher"—$850

1931, Souvenir money, Confederate $100 bill—$75

1929, Miniature ad—$100

1941, Score pad—$35

1932, Bottle bags—$15

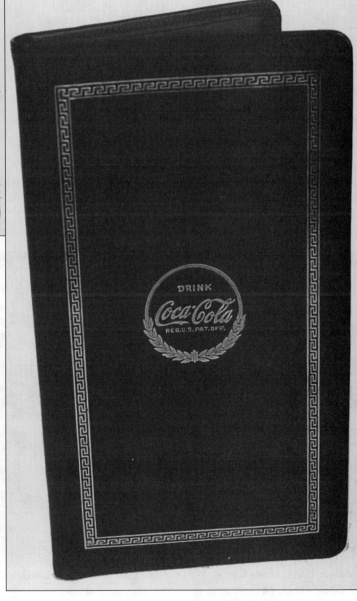

1950, Pocket secretary—$25

Menus

Item	Value
1901, Hilda Clark, 11-3/4" x 4," shown open	$1,600.00
1902, 4-1/2" x 6-1/8"	$800.00
1903, Hilda Clark, 4-1/8" x 6-1/2"	$750.00
Back of 1903 Hilda Clark menu.	
1904, Lillian Nordica, 4-1/8" x 6-1/2"	$750.00
1912, Rice paper napkin	$85.00

Menu: 1901, Hilda Clark, 11-3/4" x 4," shown open—$1,600

Menu: 1904, Lillian Nordica, 4-1/8" x 6-1/2"—$750

Menu: 1902, 4-1/2" x 6-1/8"—$800

Menu: 1903, Hilda Clark, 4-1/8" x 6-1/2"—$750

Back of 1903 Hilda Clark menu.

Menu: 1912, Rice paper napkin—$85

Serving tray, 1899, 9-1/4"—$10,000-$15,000.

1900, ceramic change receiver—$5,000.

Serving tray, 1903—$8,550.

Serving tray, 1901, Hilda Clark—$7,150.

Serving tray, 1903,
Bottle tray—$8,000.

Serving tray, 1903,
Hilda Clark—$6,250.

Vienna art plate,
1905—$425.

Vienna art plate,
1905—$500.

Serving tray, 1905,
Lillian Nordica—$4,300

Serving tray, 1906,
Juanita—$3,250

Serving tray, 1907,
Relieves Fatigue—$4,750.

Vienna art plate, 1908,
"Topless" art plate—$900.

**Serving tray, 1909,
St. Louis Fair—$4,000.**

1910, Coca-Cola girl—$1,400.

**Serving tray, 1910,
Girl at party—$500.**

**Serving tray,
1913, Oval—$800.**

**Serving tray, 1913,
Signed by Hamilton King—$1,000.**

**Serving tray, 1914,
Large oval—$850.**

**Serving tray,1917,
Elaine—$500.**

**Serving tray, 1920,
Large oval—$1,000.**

**Serving tray, 1921,
Autumn girl—$1,000.**

**Serving tray, 1922,
Summer girl—$900.**

**Serving tray, 1924,
Smiling girl—$950.**

**Serving tray, 1928,
Soda fountain clerk—$775.**

Serving tray, 1926,
Sports couple—$875.

Serving tray, 1934,
Maureen O'Sullivan—$950.

Serving tray, 1935,
Madge Evans—$440.

Serving tray, 1936,
Hostess—$450.

Serving tray, 1937,
Running girl—$360.

Serving tray, 1938,
Girl in the afternoon—$280.

Serving tray, 1940,
Sailor girl—$325.

Serving tray, 1941,
Girl ice skater—$340.

Serving tray, 1942,
Two girls at car—$370.

1961, TV tray—$35.

Sign, 1896,
Drink Delicious Refreshing—$15,000.

ICE COLD

Coca-Cola

TRADE MARK
REGISTERED

SOLD HERE

Sign, 1907,
Tin, 19" x 27"—$2,200.

DRINK

Coca-Cola

TRADE MARK
REGISTERED

DELICIOUS
AND
REFRESHING

CALL FOR IT BY FULL NAME
NICKNAMES ENCOURAGE SUBSTITUTION

Sign, 1914,
"Two Girls"—$3,650.

Sign, 1926,
small oval—$2,200.

Sign, 1927,
two-sided arrow, tin, 7-3/4" x 30"—$800.

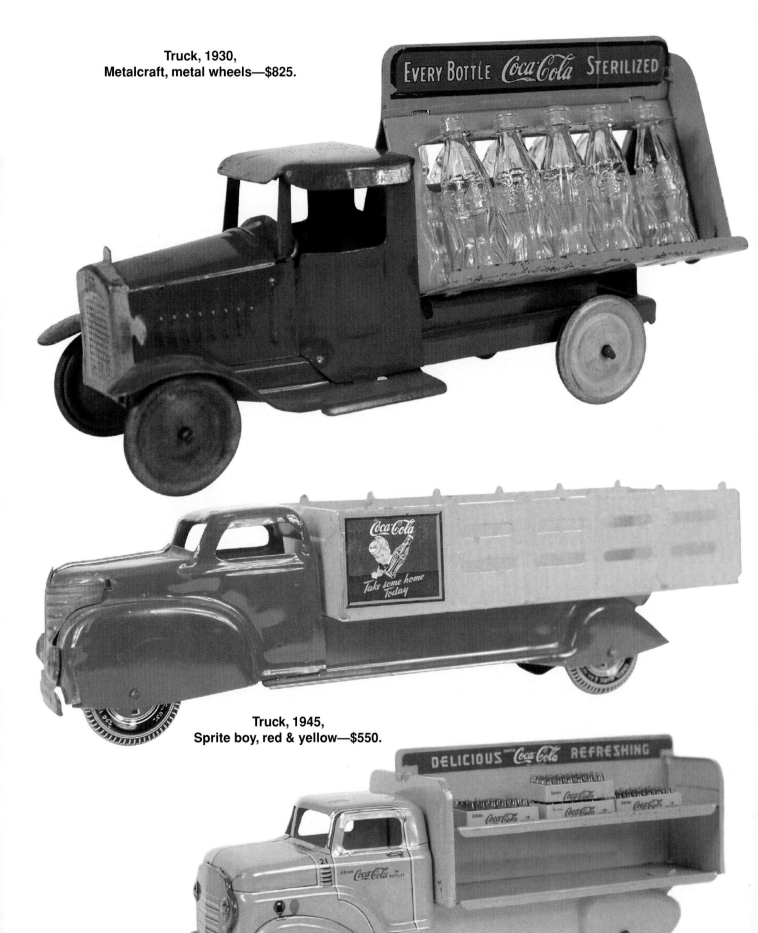

Truck, 1930,
Metalcraft, metal wheels—$825.

Truck, 1945,
Sprite boy, red & yellow—$550.

1945, Sprite boy,
yellow with red,
white & blue—$775.

VW bus, 1950,
friction motion—$275.

Truck, 1950s,
3"—$330.

1956, Drink Coca-Cola
Refreshed—$625.

1950, Open truck—$450.

1950s, Marx truck—$1,200.

1960s, Buddy L truck—$325.

1960s, Tin, Japan,
friction—$1,300.

Truck, 1960,
Buddy L—$595.

Truck, 1973—$80.

**Miniature, 1950,
dispenser bank, battery operated—$450.**

**Miniature, 1920,
embossed bottles and cases—$200.**

**Thermometer, 1941,
two bottles—$400.**

**Miniature, 1971,
king and regular size
bottles and case—$100.**

1939, Take-home carton—$175.

1940, Take-home carton—$175.

1929, Salesman's sample cooler—$5,500.

1934, Salesman's sample cooler—$3,200.

Menu, 1901,
Hilda Clark, 11-3/4" x 4," shown open—$1,600.

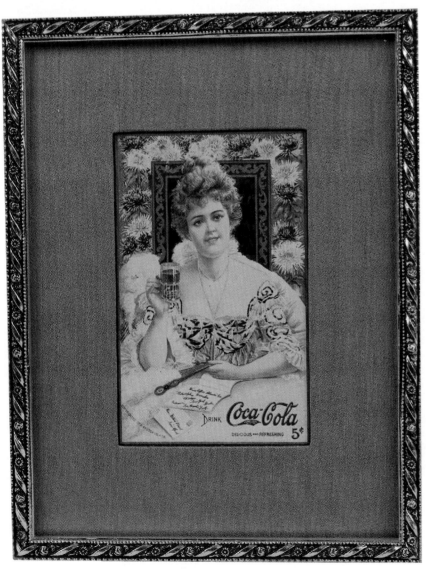

Menu, 1903,
Hilda Clark, 4-1/8" x 6-1/2"—$750.

1941, Score pad—$35.

Bookmark, 1906,
Owl—$825.

Bookmark, 1902,
Hilda Clark—$425.

Bookmark, 1903,
Lillian Nordica, 6" x 2"—$425.

Bookmark, 1904,
Lillian Russell—$525.

Bookmark, 1908,
Coca-Cola Chewing Gum, 2" x 6"—$2,000.

1891, First Coca-Cola calendar, 6-1/2" x 9", printed by Calvert Lithography Co., of Atlanta—$15,000.

Calendar, 1901,
7-3/8" x 13"—$7,500.

1904, This calendar exists with two
versions, instead of the glass on the
table, there is a bottle—$4,500.

1908, Good to the last drop (Maxwell
House later trademarked this slogan
for use with its products)—$5,500.

**1912, First calendar to use two models.
16" x 22" $5,000; 1913—$4,000.**

**1914, Betty is one of the most
popular Coca-Cola girls—$1,800.**

**1917, Issued with
glass or bottle—$2,600.**

1916, Knitting girl—$4,000.

**Calendar, 1922,
Autumn girl—$1,750.**

Calendar, 1923—$975.

Calendar, 1924—$1,300.

Calendar, 1927—$1,100.

Calendar, 1928—$1,200.

Calendar, 1929—$1,300.

**Calendar, 1932, Huckleberry Finn
by Norman Rockwell—$800.**

**Calendar, 1935,
Norman Rockwell—$775.**

1931, Farm boy with dog by Norman Rockwell, a.k.a., "Tom Sawyer"—$975.

Coupon, 1904—$400.

**Bookmark, 1903,
Lillian Nordica—$425.**

**Playing cards, 1928,
Girl with bobbed hair—$675.**

**Playing cards, 1956, Ice skater,
75th anniversary of Coca-Cola—$90.**

**Festoon, 1928,
Coca-Cola girls—$5,000.**

**Fan, 1950s,
Quality Carries On—$50.**

**Fan, 1930s,
Drink Coca-Cola—$85.**

1906, Knife and corkscrew, brass—$400.

Watch fob, 1909, brass—$300.

Pocket mirror, 1910,
Coca-Cola girl—$400.

Watch fob, 1910, celluloid (on back),
"Drink Coca-Cola in Bottles 5c"—$1,000.

Watch fob, 1912,
celluloid, 1-1/2" diameter—$2,500.

1910, Single blade
and opener—$325.

Sheet music, "The Palms"—$750.

Postcard, 1911, Duster girl—$800.

1963, Transistor radio,
7-1/2" x 3-1/2"—$300.

1963, Transistor radio, 4-1/2" x 2-1/2"—$200.

**1950,
Buddy Lee doll,
12-1/2"—$1,000.**

1950, Marbles—$35.

1940, Dominos—$60.

Playing Cards

In 1930 and 1940, Coca-Cola distributed playing cards with the same artwork used on other advertising items. Obviously, collectors prefer to collect full decks, but some playing cards have become so difficult to find that individual cards have become increasingly popular to collect.

Item	Value

1909, Coca-Cola Relieves Fatigue, girl (straight-sided bottle with straw, blue inset border, ©S.L. Whitten, Chicago, Illinois) $3,000.00

1915, Girl with parasol (Western Coca-Cola Bottling Company of Chicago offered these cards for 25 cents in stamps; the joker shows a straight-sided bottle with a paper label) $2,000.00

1928, Girl with bobbed hair (these cards have four different borders: red, light yellow, light gray and red with gold edge)...$675.00

1937-1939, Hund and Elger Bottling Co..................$????

1943, The stewardess (during the war, Coca-Cola distributed the double-deck bridge sets depicting the nurse and the switchboard operator. They sold for 33 cents to the bottlers) $100.00

1956, Ice skater commemorates 75th anniversary of Coca-Cola...$90.00

1961, Girl with a bowling ball $85.00

1963, Boy and girl at fireplace.................................$90.00

1951, The Party $100.00

1959, Sign of Good Taste $85.00

1960, Be Really Refreshed.......................................$100.00

1961, Coke Refreshed You Best $80.00

1963, Things Go Better With Coke $70.00

1963, Zing! Refreshing New Feeling.......................$75.00

1971, It's The Real Thing $20.00

1974, Drink Coca-Cola...$30.00

1976, Coca-Cola Adds Life to Everything...............$25.00

1976, Enjoy Coca-Cola $25.00

Playing cards: 1909, Coca-Cola Relieves Fatigue, girl—$3,000

Playing cards: 1943, The stewardess—$100

Playing cards: 1915, Girl with parasol—$2,000

Playing cards: 1928, Girl with bobbed hair—$675

Playing Cards

Playing cards: 1956, Ice skater, 75th anniversary of Coca-Cola—$90

Playing cards: 1961, Girl with a bowling ball—$85

Playing cards: 1963, Boy and girl at fireplace—$90

Playing cards: 1971, It's The Real Thing—$20

Playing Cards

Pocket Knives

Local bottlers distributed pocket knives since the turn-of-the-century. They incorporated single blades, double blades, openers and corkscrews.

1906, Knife and corkscrew, brass—$400

1910, Single blade and opener—$325

1920, Single blade and opener, bone.—$250

1915-1925, Single blade and opener, bone—$100

1937, Switchblade—$275

1930, One blade—$100

Item	Value
1905-1915, Double blade brass marked, "Kaster & Co." and "Coca-Cola Bottling Co."	$450.00
1905-1915, Four blades including awl, can opener and screwdriver	$500.00
1906, Knife and corkscrew, brass, single blade, marked, "Kaster & Co." and "Coca-Cola Co."	$400.00
1910, Double blade, brass, marked, "D. Peres, Solingen" and "Coca-Cola Bottling Co. Germany"	$350.00
1910, Single blade and opener marked, "D. Peres, Solingen" and "Coca-Cola Bottling Co. Germany"	$325.00
1920, Single blade and opener, bone, Kaster Bros.	$250.00
1915-1925, Single blade and opener, bone, "A. Kaster & Bros., New York"	$100.00
1915, Double blade, copper, marked, "A. Kastor & Bros., NY"	$250.00
1937, Switchblade	$275.00
1930, Compliments the Coca-Cola	$100.00
1930, One blade	$100.00
1940s, "Serve Coca-Cola," single blade and nail file	$190.00
1930, Double blade, celluloid, "Shapleigh HDW, Co."	$100.00
1930, Double blade, celluloid, "Hammer Brand, USA"	$65.00
1930, Double blade, stainless, "Remington UMC"	$125.00
1930, Double blade, stainless, "Coca-Cola Co., Atlanta"	$125.00
1930, Double blade, stainless, "Remington"	$150.00
1930, Double blade, stainless, "Coca-Cola Bottling Co., Germany"	$75.00
1930, Single blade with corkscrew, pearl, "Pure as Sunlight"	$125.00
1935, Double blade, celluloid, "Drink Coca-Cola in Bottles"	$125.00
1935, Single blade with corkscrew, pearl, "Colonial Prov. R.I."	$75.00

1930, Compliments the Coca-Cola—$100

1940s, "Serve Coca-Cola," single blade and nail file—$190

Pocket Mirrors

Women frequently carried pocket mirrors because they could be conveniently stored in their purses. There are many reproductions, but they are easy to spot once you've seen an original. Information shown in quotation marks is the copy as written on the bottom or side rim of the mirror. This is the easiest way to identify an original. Before 1913, all pocket mirrors came with the following copy: "Duplicate Mirrors 5c Postage, Coca-Cola Company, Atlanta, Ga."

Item	Value
1907, Relieves Fatigue, "From the Painting Copyright 1906, by Wolf & Co. Phila. Bastian Bros. Co. Roch. N.Y."	$600.00
1909, St. Louis, "J.B. Carroll Chicago"	$575.00
1906, Juanita, "The Whitehead & Hoag Co., Newark, NJ"	$600.00
1910, Coca-Cola girl, "J.B. Carroll Chicago"	$400.00
1911, Coca-Cola girl, "The Whitehead & Hoag Co. Newark, N.J."	$400.00
1914, Oval	$665.00
1916, Elaine, "The Whitehead & Hoag Co. Newark, N.J."	$500.00
1920, Garden girl, "Bastian Bros. Co. Rochester, N.Y."	$825.00
1922, Bathing suit girl, "The Whitehead & Hoag Co. Newark, N.J."	$3,750.00
1936, 50th Anniversary	$125.00

Pocket mirror: 1920, Garden girl—$825

Pocket mirror: 1909, St. Louis—$575

Pocket mirror: 1910, Coca-Cola girl—$400

Pocket mirror: 1914, oval—$665

Pocket mirror: 1907, Relieves Fatigue—$600

Pocket mirror: 1936, 50th Anniversary—$125

Postcards

Postcard: 1909, Bottling plant—$50

Item	Value
1909, Bottling plant	$50.00
1910, Bottling plant	$250.00
1910, The Coca-Cola girl	$800.00
1911, Duster girl	$800.00
1913, Delivery wagon	$100.00
1915, Delivery wagon	$100.00
1942, Dick Tracy	$100.00
1940s, All Over The World	$550.00
1940s, Gaining	$500.00
1940s, Have You a Hobby	$525.00
1940s, Your Profits	$500.00
1940s, You Can Figure It Out Yourself	$550.00

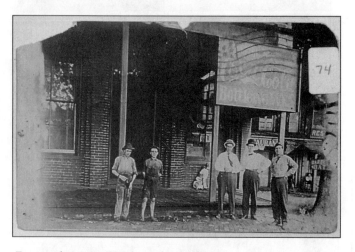

Postcard: 1910, Bottling plant—$250

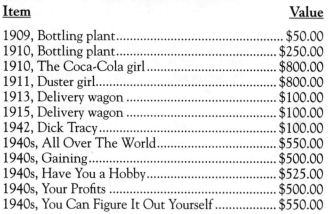

Postcard: 1911, Duster girl—$800

Postcard: 1910, The Coca-Cola girl—$800

Postcard: 1913, delivery wagon—$100

Postcard: 1915, delivery wagon—$100

Postcard: 1942, Dick Tracy—$100

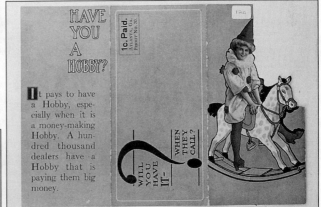

Postcard: 1940s, Have You a Hobby—$525

Postcard: 1940s, All Over
The World—$550

Postcard: 1911, Duster
girl—$800

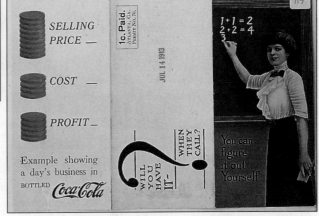

Postcard: 1940s, You Can Figure It Out Yourself—$550

Radio Advertising

Many of Coca-Cola's first radio spots were recorded on disks that are widely traded and collected. Coca-Cola began its radio advertising in 1927 with a 14-week program about the romance between Vivian, the first Coca-Cola girl, and Jim.

In 1930, Coca-Cola began sponsoring a radio show featuring celebrity hosts. This show expanded in 1934 and 1935. Complete with a 65-piece orchestra and a 25-member vocal group, "The Pause That Refreshes" was a half-hour of popular music with three Coca-Cola advertisements.

Until the appearance of television in the early 1950s, Coca-Cola sponsored a wide variety of radio programs. One memorable show began in November of 1941 and was called "Spotlight Bands." The show featured a series of different bands selected to entertain young Americans in the Armed Forces. Other programs featured such radio and music stars as Percy Faith, Spike Jones, Edgar Bergen with Charlie McCarthy and Mario Lanza.

Although Coca-Cola began to focus more on television advertising in the 1950s, it had its greatest radio hit in 1970 with a song called, "I'd Like to Buy the World a Coke." The song was so successful that Coca-Cola revised and changed the title to, "I'd Like to teach the World to Sing." The two versions sold more than a million copies with all the proceeds going to UNICEF.

Because there are people who save only old radio serials, it is possible to find and own a nice collection of Coca-Cola broadcasts.

Item	Value
1930, Bottle radio, 24" (price is for all original parts in original near mint condition)	$5,000.00
1949, Cooler radio, 7" x 12" x 9-1/2"	$850.00
1950, Crystal radio set	$300.00
1963, Transistor radio, vending machine shape, 7-1/2" x 3-1/2"	$300.00
1963, Transistor radio, vending machine shape, 4-1/2" x 2-1/2"	$200.00
1971, Coke can radio	$35.00
1972, Transistor radio	$150.00

1930, Bottle radio, 24"—$5,000

1949, Cooler radio, 7" x 12" x 9-1/2"—$850

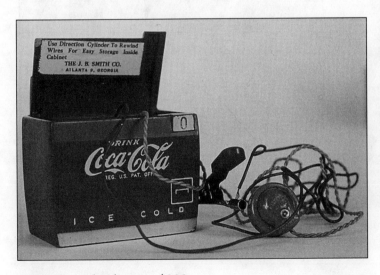

1950, Crystal radio set—$300

1963, Transistor radio, 7-1/2" x 3-1/2"—$200

1963, Transistor radio, 4-1/2" x 2-1/2"—$300

1971, Coke can radio—$35

1972, Transistor radio—$150

Records & Sheet Music

Records

Item	Value
1945, Salesman training record, 33-1/3 rpm (used for training employees)	$20.00
1950s, Morton Downey record	$25.00
1950s, Eddie Fisher, 45 rpm	$20.00
1951, Tony Bennett record	$25.00
1962, "Anita Bryant Refreshing New Feeling," 33-1/3 rpm	$35.00
1963, "Here and Now," 45 rpm	$15.00
1965, "Sue Thompson Swings The Jingle," 33-1/3 rpm	$40.00
1967, "Trini Lopez," 45 rpm	$15.00
1968, "Camelot," Los Angles Bottling Co., 45 rpm	$10.00
1970s, ... Original radio broadcasts. These were actual old radio shows that were part of the afternoon series. Coca-Cola advertisements appear on the back of the albums.	
W.C. Fields	$30.00
The Lone Ranger	$30.00
Sgt. Preston of The Yukon	$30.00
Dick Tracy	$30.00
Superman	$30.00
1971, "It's The Real Thing"	$15.00

1945, Salesman training record, 33-1/3 rpm—$20

1950s, Morton Downey record—$25

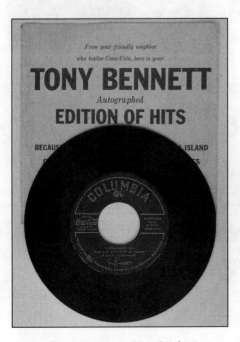

1951, Tony Bennett record—$25

1963, "Here and Now," 45 rpm—$15

1970s, W.C. Fields—$30

1970s, W.C. Fields—$30

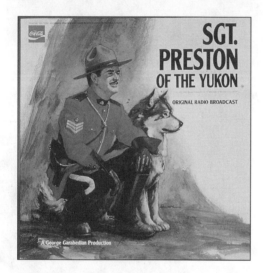

1970s, Sgt. Preston of The Yukon—$30

1970s, Dick Tracy—$30

1970s, Superman—$30

1971, "It's The Real Thing"—$15

Records & Sheet Music

Sheet Music

Item	Value

1906, Juanita sheet music set, 10-1/4" x 13-1/4", lithographed in Germany

"The Palms" $750.00
"My Old Kentucky Home" $750.00
"Rock Me To Sleep Mother" $750.00
"Ben Bolt" $750.00

Also available but not pictured

"Juanita" $1,000.00
"My Coca-Cola Bride" $750.00
"Old Folks At Home" $750.00
"Lead Kindly Light" $750.00
"Nearer, My God To Thee" $750.00

1912, "When The Do-Do Bird is Singing in The Coca-Cola Tree" $575.00

1913, "My Coco-Cola Belle," misspelled cover, inside spelled "Coca-Cola" $350.00

1915, "Follow Me Girls to the Fountain and Be My Coca-Cola Girl," 10-3/4" x 13-3/4" $625.00

1927, Sheet music, The Coca-Cola girl, 7-1/2" x 12-1/2" $275.00

1942, "Theme Song for The Coca-Cola Company" $75.00

1940s, "Rum and Coca-Cola," 10-1/2" x 13", Jeri Sullavan $35.00

1940s, "Rum and Coca-Cola," 10-1/2" x 13", The Andrew Sisters $25.00

1944, "Rum and Coca-Cola," 10-1/2" x 13", French Version $75.00

1941, "We Stand United" $45.00

1955, "50 Million Times a Day" $95.00

1971, "I'd Like to Buy the World a Coke" $20.00

1971, "It's The Real Thing" $20.00

Sheet music: "The Palms"—$750

Sheet music: "My Old Kentucky Home"—$750

Sheet music: "Ben Bolt"—$750

Sheet music: "Rock Me To Sleep Mother"—$750

Sheet music: 1927, The Coca-Cola girl, 7-1/2" x 12-1/2"—$275

Sheet music: 1971, "I'd Like to Buy the World a Coke"—$20

Sheet music: 1971, "It's The Real Thing"—$20

St. Nicholas

The Bishop of Myra lived in the country of Lycia (located in Asia Minor) around 300 A.D. This gentle-natured man, with his great dedication to children and mankind, was the basis for the legend of St. Nicholas. In 1882, Clement Clarke Moore's poem "'Twas the Night Before Christmas" promoted the image of St. Nicholas as that of a pixie-like character.

The image of Santa Claus changed over the years. By 1931, the artist Haddon Sundblom had developed a realistic portrait of Santa Claus that would be used in Christmas advertisements for years to come. Some characteristics of Haddon's Santa were white hair and a lengthy beard, a long red coat trimmed in white fur, a leather belt with a buckle and high boots.

Santa Claus memorabilia can make a very fascinating collection. The following slogans connected Santa and Coca-Cola on cards, billboards, magazine advertisements, blotters, etc.

Year	Item
1930	The Busiest man in the World comes up smiling after…the pause that refreshes (first advertisement for Coca-Cola with Santa Claus in it)
1932	Please Pause Here, Jimmy
1933	Away with a tired face. Bounce back to normal (Santa taking off a tired yawning face)
1934	The Pause That Keeps You Going
1935	It Will Refresh You Too
1936	Me Too. The Pause That Refreshes.
1937	Give And Take, Say I (Santa drinking a bottle of Coke and eating a piece of chicken from someone's refrigerator)
1938	Thanks For the Pause That Refreshes

Year	Item
1939	And the Same to You
1940	Someone Knew I Was Coming
1941	Thirst Asks Nothing More
1943	Drink Coca-Cola
1944	Here's to G.I. Joes
1945	They Knew What I Wanted
1946	For Me
1947	Busy Man's Pause
1948	Hospitality
1950	For Santa
1951	Now It's My Time
1955	Almost Everyone Appreciates the Best
1956	'Twas the Night Before Christmas
1958	Santa's Pause (Santa taking off his boots)

1932, Please Pause Here, Jimmy

School Supplies

Originally, because of the caffeine content, Coca-Cola never advertised to children. As Coca-Cola began to target the youth for consumption of their popular beverage, Coca-Cola began to distribute its advertising materials in schools. Coke produced pencils, pens, rulers, sharpeners, erasers, tablets, book covers and educational materials. Because Coca-Cola gave away educational items to so many schools in such large quantities, they are abundant and accessible for today's collectors.

Item	Value
30-1. 1925, Book cover	$55.00
30-2. 1951, Book cover, distributed to school bookstores to be given to book purchasers	$20.00
30-5. 1950, Paper writing pad, "Safety ABCs"	$20.00
30-6. 1960, Paper writing pad, "Flags of the United Nation"	$20.00
30-7. 1960, Paper writing pad, "Landmarks of the USA"	$20.00
30-8. 1930, Pencil box	$65.00
30-9. 1930s, Pencil sharpener, cast-iron	$50.00
30-10. 1950s, Plastic pencil sharpener	$30.00
30-11. 1960s, Mechanical pencil	$35.00
30-12. 1940s, Golden Rule ruler ....., "Do Unto Others As You Would Have Them Do Unto You" Yard Stick (This ruler, completely unchanged, has been given out for over 45 years.)	$5.00
30-3. 1929-1934, Nature study cards, set consists of 8 series of 12 cards	
Complete set in box, 96 cards	$100.00
Individual series, 12 cards	$8.00
Individual cards	$1.00
Small set consists of 2 series of 12 cards, each	$18.00

1925, book cover—$55

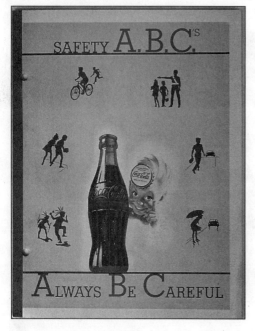

1950, paper writing pad, "Safety ABCs"—$20

1951, book cover, distributed to school bookstores—$20

1950s, plastic pencil sharpener—$30

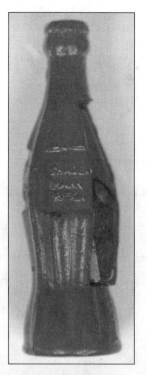

1960, paper writing pad, "Flags of the United Nation"—$20

1930s, pencil sharpener, cast-iron—$50

1960s, mechanical pencil—$35

1940s, Golden Rule ruler—$5

1960, paper writing pad, "Landmarks of the USA"—$20

1930, pencil box—$65

1929-1934, Nature study cards, complete set—$100

1943, America's Fighting Planes. These were produced when schools were having regular air raid drills. They were provided to schools to help teach children how to spot enemy planes. The following list provides the name of the fighting plane so you can better identify it.

Set No. 1—complete set $125
1. Grumman F4F-3
2. Ryan Low-Wing Trainer PT-21
3. Curtis P-40
4. Vultec Vengeance
5. Bill Aircobra
6. North American B-25
7. Consolodated PBY
8. Boeing Flying Fortress B-17D
9. Glenn L. Martin B-26
10. Lockheed P-38
11. Voight F4V-1
12. Douglas A-20-A

Set No. 2—complete set $125
1. Douglas B-19
2. Consolodated PBY2Y-2
3. Consolodated PBY-5
4. Voight-Sikorsky
5. Boeing B-17E
6. Consolodated B-24
7. North American B-25
8. Douglas SBD
9. Grumman F4-4
10. Brewster SB2A-1
11. Curtiss G-1
12. Grumman TBF-1
13. Republic P-47

14. Douglas A-20
15. Martin B-26
16. Lockheed P-38
17. Waco Glider CG-YA
18. Bill P-39
19. Curtiss P-40F
20. Vultec Trainer

Set No. 3—complete set $125
1. North American A-36 "Invader"
2. Lockheed P-38 "Lightening"
3. Republic P-47 "Thunderbolt"
4. Bill P-39 "Aircobra"
5. Curtiss P-40 "Warhawk"
6. Douglas P-70 "Havoc"
7. Boeing B-17 "Fortress"
8. Consolodated B-24 "Liberator"
9. North American B-25 "Mitchell"
10. Martin B-26 "Marauder"
11. Grumman F6F "Hellcat"
12. Grumman F4F …"Wildcat"
13. Voight-Sikorsky F4V "Corsair"
14. Curtiss SB2C "Helldiver"
15. Grumman TBF "Avenger"
16. Martin PMM "Mariner"
17. Consolodated PBY "Catalina"
18. Voight-Sikorsky OS2U "Kingfisher"
19. Voight-Sikorsky YR4 "Helicopter"
20. Lockheed C-69 "Constellation"

1943, America's Fighting Planes

Signs

Coca-Cola invested a large percentage of its advertising budget toward sign production. The signs came in many shapes and sizes and were made of cloth, paper, cardboard, metal, glass and wood. The signs started simply, using just the name Coca-Cola; then, pictures of bottles and glasses were added. Later, they depicted the beautiful people who drank the fast growing product. They were used to decorate stores and public areas, as well as being placed on public streets and in public transportation. Some were made to be temporary while others were made to last forever.

Cloth or canvas signs were the basic start for the message that would soon travel the country. The message was simple with a plain graphic. Today, these banners are produced in plastic and still used at stores and gas stations.

The versatility of cardboard signs made them abundant for display indoors as well as outdoors. Their sturdy material made it possible to hang or incorporate them into a free standing display. Rectangular signs have been used repeatedly to promote Coca-Cola. Originally they were used to advertise on streetcars. During a time when most of the world commuted on streetcars, these elaborate ads lined the inside of the cars. Later, they produced special frames to use with these cardboard inserts inside of stores. Some of the most unique and unusual cardboard signs are the cutouts. Irregular die-cut cardboard signs showed men, women and nature at its best.

Festoons are several cardboard cutouts held together by either grommets or ribbons. They can adapt to the size of the space depending on how they are hung. They started out simply spelling the word Coca-Cola. Typically they portrayed a beautiful woman adorned by picturesque flowers, but later included many subjects. These festoons were used to decorate store front windows, as well as provide a back bar display.

Metal signs were manufactured for sturdy outdoor use, as well as many shapes and sizes for indoor use. Originally these signs were uncomplicated, having only a few colors and a simple message that could be read from afar. The company produced heavy-duty porcelain signs for extended use, as well as tin-plated signs for a shorter life span. The signs progressed to hanging two-way or free-standing signs outside a store. Indoor metal signs were smaller and more specific in nature. They usually included both a woman and the product displayed in full color.

Item	Value
1896, Drink Delicious Refreshing	$15,000.00
1900, Bottle, celluloid	$3,700.00
1899, Hilda Clark, 20" x 28"	$15,000.00
1900, Hilda Clark, paper, 15" x 20"	$8,500.00
1903, Hilda Clark, 15" x 18-1/2"	$16,000.00
1904, Lillian Nordica, 8-1/2" x 11" (cardboard sign covered by celluloid, plastic-like material, that protects paper underneath)	$9,000.00
1905, Lillian Nordica cameo, 19" x 25", celluloid-covered cardboard	$12,000.00
1905, Lillian Nordica, 26" x 46"	$10,000.00
1904, St. Louis Fair, cardboard, 28-1/2" x 45"	$13,000.00
1907, Tin, 19" x 27"	$2,200.00
1908, Cherub, 14-3/4"	$5,000.00
1912, 16" x 24," printed by Ketterlinus Co., Phila., Pa.	$6,000.00
1914, "Two Girls"	$3,650.00
1914, Betty, tin, 31" x 41" (one of the largest metal signs ever made for indoor use, manufactured by the Passaic Metal Ware Co.)	$6,000.00
1915, Cardboard	$4,000.00
1917, Elaine, tin, 20" x 30-1/2"	$5,500.00
1920, Coca-Cola in bottles, 17" chrome radiator plate	$500.00

Item	Value
1920, Glass	$1,000.00
1920, Paper signs	
Pause a Minute-Refresh Yourself	$825.00
That Taste Good Feeling	$900.00
Treat Yourself Right, 12" x 20"	$800.00
An Ice Cold With a Red Hot, 10" x 30"	$975.00
Off to a Fresh Start, 10" x 30"	$1,150.00
Ice Cold	$850.00
Drink Coca-Cola	$725.00
Great Get Together	$700.00
Between Bites	$700.00
Some Treat	$825.00
1926, Large oval, 13" x 19"	$5,000.00
1926, Small oval, 8" x 11"	$2,200.00
1920s-30s, Reverse glass mirror, 11-1/4" diameter	$650.00
1927, Two-sided arrow, tin, 7-3/4" x 30"	$800.00
1931, Tin sign, 4-1/2" x 12-1/2", embossed	$500.00
1933, Bottle tin, embossed	$1,000.00
1935, Wooden sign, 19" x 20" (plywood sign made by Kay Displays, Inc.)	$1,075.00
1940, Plastic sign with bottle, wood with metal trim	$475.00
1950, Porcelain sign, 3 ft.	$750.00

Sign: 1896, Drink Delicious Refreshing—
$15,000

Sign: 1900, bottle, celluloid—$3,700

Sign: 1899, Hilda Clark, 20" x 28"—$15,000

Sign: 1900, Hilda Clark, paper, 15" x 20"—$8,500

Sign: 1903, Hilda Clark, tin, 15" x 18-1/2"—$16,000

Sign: 1904, Lillian Nordica, 8-1/2" x 11", celluloid-covered cardboard—$5,000

Sign: 1905, Lillian Nordica, 19" x 25", celluloid-covered cardboard—$12,000

Sign: 1905, Lillian Nordica, 26" x 46"—$10,000

Sign: 1907, Tin, 19" x 27"—$2,200

Sign: 1908, Cherub, 14-3/4"—$5,000

Sign: 1912, 16" x 24"—$6,000

Sign: 1915, cardboard—$4,000

Sign: 1914, Betty, tin, 31" x 41"—$6,000

Sign: 1914, "Two Girls"—$3,650

Sign: 1917, Elaine, tin, 20" x 30-1/2"—$5,500

Sign: 1920, glass—$1,000

Sign: 1920, Coca-Cola in bottles,
17" chrome radiator plate—$500

Sign: 1926, large oval, 13" x 19"—$5,000

Sign: small oval, 8" x 11"—$2,200

Sign: 1931, tin, 4-1/2" x 12-1/2", embossed—$500

Sign: 1920s-30s, reverse glass mirror, 11-1/4" diameter—$650

Sign: 1927, two-sided arrow, tin, 7-3/4" x 30"—$800

Sign: 1935, wood, 19" x 20"—$1,075

Sign: 1950, porcelain sign, 3 ft.—$750

Sign: 1940, plastic sign with bottle, wood with metal trim—$475

Smoking Paraphernalia

186Match safes and holders were useful and elegant for carrying wooden matches but expensive to manufacture. Later, paper matches were produced easily and inexpensively. However, they were less durable and are more difficult to find.

Item	Value
1906, Matchbook holder	$350.00
1907, Matchbook holder	$375.00
1908, Match safe brass	$425.00
1910, Celluloid matchbook holder	$350.00
1930s, Cigar band	$250.00
1936, Cigarette box, frosted glass, Fiftieth Anniversary	$725.00
1936, Fiftieth Anniversary solid brass ashtray	$42.00
1940, Four-suit ashtrays ruby red glass	$450.00
1940, Match holder ashtray, pullmatch	$1,200.00
1950, Bottle lighter	$28.00
1950, Crinkled ashtray, aluminum	$13.00
1960, Musical lighter	$65.00
1950, Can lighter	$60.00
1960s, Miniature lighter	$27.00

1908, Match safe brass—$425

1907, Matchbook holder—$375

1907, Matchbook holder—$350

1950, Bottle lighter—$28

1910, Celluloid matchbook holder—$350

1936, Cigarette box, frosted glass,
Fiftieth Anniversary—$725

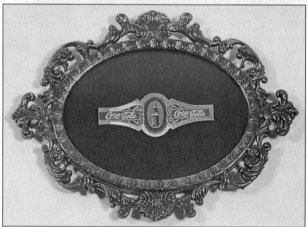

1930s, Cigar band—$250

1936, Fiftieth Anniversary solid brass ashtray—$42

1940, Four-suit ashtrays
ruby red glass—$450

1940, Match holder ashtray, pullmatch—
$1,200

1950, Can lighter—$60

1960s, Miniature lighter—$27

1950, Crinkled ashtray, aluminum—$13

Assorted Matches

Smoking Paraphernalia

1950, Ashtray with bottle lighter—$155

Matches

Item	Value
1908, Ask For a Bottle	$1,000.00
1912, Drink Coca-Cola in Bottles	$750.00
1913, Drink Delicious Coca-Cola	$750.00
1914, Drink Coca-Cola	$650.00
1920, A Distinctive Drink in Distinctive Bottle...	$500.00
1930, A Pure Drink	$25.00
1950, Take Home a Carton	$25.00
1964, World's Fair, New York	$25.00

Ashtrays

Item	Value
1950, Ashtray with bottle lighter	$155.00
1960, Drink Coca-Cola	$12.00
1960, Drink Coca-Cola	$12.00
1960, Things Go Better With Coke	$10.00
1960s, Glass ashtray	$10.00

1960, Drink Coca-Cola—$12

1960, Things Go Better With Coke—$10

1960, Drink Coca-Cola—$12

1960s, Glass ashtray—$10

Sports Items

During the summer of 1928 in Amsterdam, Coca-Cola aligned itself with the Olympics, and Coca-Cola was served to the spectators. Once Coca-Cola began its partnership with the Olympics, the linking of sports and Coca-Cola became common. Coke advertised on bowling score sheets, baseball scorekeepers, baseball rules booklets, sports programs and boating guides. The famous logo might be associated with softball, hockey, horse racing, cricket, football, basketball and bowling, but baseball leads the list for available collectibles.

Item	Value
1907, Baseball scorekeeper, celluloid "Perpetual Counter"	$165.00
1932, Olympic record indicator	$150.00
1960, Hall of Fame records American and National Leagues	$75.00
1968, Baseball bat, wood	$135.00

Coca-Cola Baseball Inserts: These inserts were placed in cartons during 1952. They retail for $85 each or $1,000 set of 10. Included in the set are:

Wes Westrum, Giants; Gil Hodges, Dodgers; Bobby Thompson, Giants; Hank Bauer, Yankees; Gil McDougal, Yankees; Ed Lopat, Yankees; Bobby Thompson, Giants; Pee Wee Reese, Dodgers; Don Mueller, Giants; Carl Furillo, Dodgers

Baseball Cards

Item	Value
1916, Chicago & St. Louis	$250.00
1942, St. Louis Cardinals	$25.00
1942, St. Louis Browns	$30.00
1949, Cardinals	$15.00
1952, Pittsburgh Pirates	$12.00
1957, Dodgers	$15.00
1960, Orioles	$10.00
1963, Mets	$10.00
1964, Red Sox	$10.00
1966, Red Sox	$10.00

1907, Baseball scorekeeper, celluloid "Perpetual Counter"—$165

1932, Olympic record indicator—$150

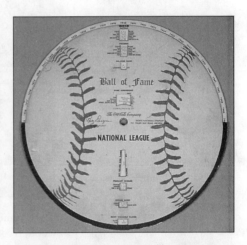

1960, Hall of Fame records American and National Leagues—$75

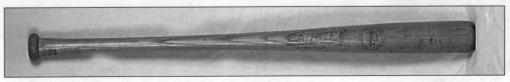

1968, Baseball bat, wood—$135

Thermometers

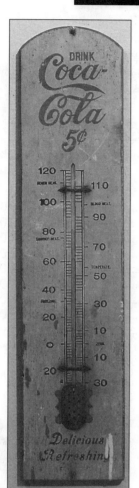

Thermometer: 1905, wood, 4" x 15"—$435

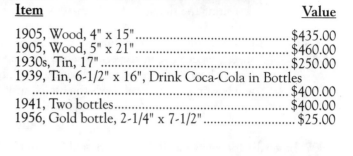

Item	Value
1905, Wood, 4" x 15"	$435.00
1905, Wood, 5" x 21"	$460.00
1930s, Tin, 17"	$250.00
1939, Tin, 6-1/2" x 16", Drink Coca-Cola in Bottles	$400.00
1941, Two bottles	$400.00
1956, Gold bottle, 2-1/4" x 7-1/2"	$25.00

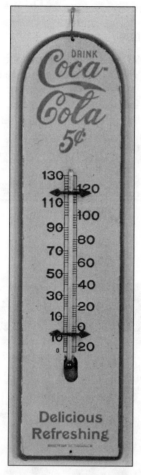

Thermometer: 1905, wood, 5" x 21"—$460

Thermometer: 1939, tin, 6-1/2" x 16", Drink Coca-Cola in Bottles—$400

Thermometer: 1930s, tin, 17"—$250

Thermometer: 1941, two bottles—$400

Thermometer: 1956, gold bottle, 2-1/4" x 7-1/2"—$25

Toys

Coca-Cola toys and games are plentiful. Toy manufacturers worldwide produced many toys with the Coca-Cola trademark, but without the company's approval. As a result, in 1980, Coca-Cola finalized a licensing program. However, the company did produce things such as playing cards and games to promote the sale of Coca-Cola.

From 1940 to 1960, the Milton Bradley Company of Springfield, Mass., manufactured games that were usually packaged in red boxes. The list of games produced includes backgammon, bingo, checkers, chess, cribbage, darts, dominoes, ring toss and tic-tac-toe. While these games were usually distributed to schools, churches, clubs and hospitals, during World War II, the company and bottlers also distributed these games to military bases.

Item	Value
1930, 3-wheel scooter	$2,500.00
1930, American Flyer kite	$325.00
1930, Bingo	$35.00
1930, Circus cutouts, with glass (comes also with bottle)	$125.00
1930, Checkers	$125.00
1930, Cribbage board	$75.00
1930, Jump rope, "Pure As Sunlight"	$375.00
1930, Toonerville town	$250.00
1930, Toy town	$125.00
1930, Wood top	$400.00
1930s, Punchboard, 9-1/4" x 9-1/4"	$1,100.00
1935, Dart board	$125.00
1938, Steps to health game	$85.00
1938, Toy stove	$1,800.00
1938, Toy train car	$1,500.00
1940, Boomerang	$30.00
1940, Chinese checkers	$150.00
1940, Darts	$75.00
1940, Dominos	$60.00
1940s, (Milton Berle) Bingo	$65.00
1940s, (Milton Berle) Broadsides	$65.00
1940s, (Milton Berle) Chess set	$85.00
1940s, (Milton Berle) Darts	$50.00
1940s, (Milton Berle) Dominoes	$50.00
1940s, (Milton Berle) Jigsaw puzzle	$300.00
1940s, (Milton Berle) Ring toss	$165.00
1940, Tic-Tac-Toe	$150.00
1940, Table tennis	$110.00
1940, Tower of Hanoi games	$200.00
1940, Whistle	$55.00
1940, Winko baseball board game	$300.00
1950, Buddy Lee doll, 12-1/2"	$1,000.00
1950, Marbles	$35.00
1950, Model plane	$75.00
1950, Ping-Pong paddles	$110.00
1950, Telescope	$185.00
1951, Comic book	$65.00
1950s, Shanghai game	$30.00
1960, Bang gun	$50.00
1960, Bingo	$3.00
1960, Dispenser	$100.00
1960, Puzzle	$35.00

Item	Value
1960, Rocking horse	$220.00
1960, Santa, 16", black patent leather boots	$200.00
1960, Yo-yo	$12.00
1968, Puzzle in a can	$35.00
1965, Magic	$225.00
1970, Frisbee	$20.00
1970, Santa, white boots	$150.00
1971, Beanbag	$25.00

1930, American Flyer kite—$325

1930, Bingo—$35

1930, Circus cutouts, with glass
(comes also with bottle)—$125

1930, Checkers—$125

1930, Cribbage board—$75

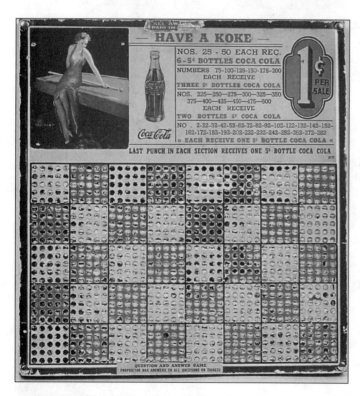

1930s, Punchboard, 9-1/4" x 9-1/4"—$1,100

1938, Toy stove—$1,800

Toys

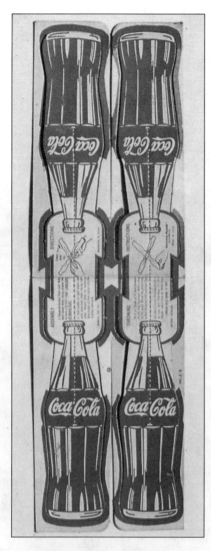

1940, Boomerang—$30

1938, Toy train car—$1,500

1940, Darts—$75

1940, Dominos—$60.

1940, Tic-Tac-Toe—$150

1950, Model plane—$75

1950, Marbles—$35

1950, Buddy Lee doll, 12-1/2"—$1,000

1950, Ping-Pong paddles—$110

1960, Bingo—$3

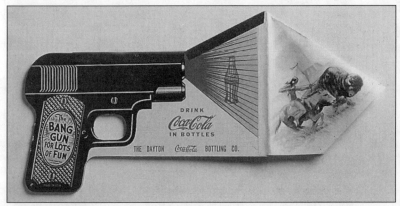

1960, Bang gun—$50

1960, Santa, 16", black patent leather boots—$200

Toys

1960, Yo-yo—$12

1965, Magic—$225

1970, Frisbee—$20

1971, Beanbag—$25

Trays

Trays used to advertise Coca-Cola can be divided into three general categories depending on their intended use: serving trays, change trays and TV trays. Serving trays were used to serve bottles or glasses of Coke. Change trays were used to give change back to the customer. Because tips were left on these change trays, they are sometimes referred to as "tip trays." TV trays were used to eat your dinner in front of the TV.

J.F. Meek started the manufacturing of Coca-Cola trays and finalized his company in 1909 under the name of American Art Works. The following is a list of manufacturers that produced trays during this transitional period:

Sentenne & Green: 1899
Standard Advertising Company: 1900
The Meek and Beach Company: 1901, 1905
Charles W. Shonk Company: 1903, 1907
N.Y. Metal Ceiling Company: 1906
H.D. Beach Company: 1909, 1922
American Art Works: 1910, 1923-42
Stelad Signs-Passaic Metal Ware Company: 1913-14, 1916
Tindeco: 1927, 1929

Tray shapes started as round, but progressed quickly to also include oval and rectangular-shaped trays. No one knows how many of each tray was produced originally, but two million trays were distributed annually. Most trays showed a glass until fountain use declined and bottle use increased. After 1930, all trays depicted Coca-Cola in bottles.

Change Trays

Item	Value
1903	$1,800.00
1904, St. Louis Fair	$650.00
1906, 4-1/4" x 6"	$900.00
1906, 4" diameter	$900.00
1913	$600.00
1914, Betty	$500.00
1917, Elaine	$300.00
1920, Garden girl	$475.00

Change tray: 1903—$1,800

Change tray: 1904, St. Louis Fair—$650

Change tray: 1906, 4-1/4" x 6"—$900

Change tray: 1906, 4" diameter—$900

Change tray: 1913—$600

Change tray: 1917, Elaine—$300

Change tray: 1914, Betty—$500

Change tray: 1920, Garden girl—$475

Serving Trays

Item	Value
1897, Victorian girl	$25,000.00
1899, 9-1/4"	$15,000.00
1900, Hilda Clark (border decorated with cola nuts and cocoa leaves)	$8,500.00
1901, Hilda Clark	$7,150.00
1903, Bottle tray	$8,000.00
1903, 15" x 18-1/2"	$8,550.00
1903, Hilda Clark	$6,250.00
1905, Lillian Nordica	$4,300.00
1906, Juanita	$3,250.00
1907, Relieves Fatigue	$4,750.00
1909, St. Louis Fair	$4,000.00
1910, Coca-Cola girl	$1,400.00
1910, Girl at party	$500.00
1913, Signed by Hamilton King	$1,000.00
1913, Oval	$800.00
1914, Betty	$800.00
1914, Large oval	$850.00
1916, Elaine	$500.00
1920, Garden girl	$975.00
1920, Large oval	$1,000.00
1922, Summer girl	$900.00
1923, Flapper girl	$500.00
1921, Autumn girl	$1,000.00
1924, Smiling girl	$950.00
1926, Sports couple	$875.00
1927, Curb service	$800.00
1927, Girl with bobbed hair	$775.00
1928, Soda fountain clerk	$775.00

Item	Value
1929, Girl in swimsuit holding glass	$525.00
1929, Girl in swimsuit holding bottle	$525.00
1930, Bathing beauty	$660.00
1930, Girl with a telephone	$475.00
1931, Farm boy with dog	$940.00
1932, Bathing beauty	$810.00
1933, Francis Dee	$625.00
1934, Maureen O'Sullivan	$950.00
1935, Madge Evans	$440.00
1936, Hostess	$450.00
1937, Running girl	$360.00
1938, Girl in the afternoon	$280.00
1939, Springboard girl	$310.00
1940, Sailor girl	$325.00
1941, Girl ice skater	$345.00
1942, Two girls at car	$370.00
1950s, Girl with wind in her hair	$100.00
1953, Girl with menu	$85.00
1953, Same tray in French	$100.00
1957, Birdhouse tray	$200.00
1957, Girl with the umbrella	$325.00
1957, Rooster tray	$150.00
1961, Pansy garden, Be Really Refreshed	$35.00
1961, Pansy garden, Coke Refreshes You Best	$35.00
1968, Lillian Russell	$60.00
1968, Lillian Russell, same tray in French	$60.00
1969, Lillian Nordica	$35.00
1971, 1909 reproduction	$5.00

Serving tray: 1897, Victorian girl. In this condition, value is $12,000, with one in mint condition at $25,000

Serving tray: 1899, 9-1/4". In this condition, value is $10,000, with one in mint condition at $15,000

Serving tray: 1900, Hilda Clark—$8,500

Serving tray: 1901, Hilda Clark—$7,150

Serving tray: 1903, Bottle tray—$8,000

Serving tray: 1903, 15" x 18-1/2"—$8,550

Serving tray: 1903, Hilda Clark—$6,250

Serving tray: 1905, Lillian Nordica—$4,300

Serving tray: 1906, Juanita—$3,250

Serving tray: 1907, Relieves Fatigue—$4,750

Serving tray: 1909, St. Louis Fair—$4,000

Serving tray: 1910, Coca-Cola girl—$1,400

Serving tray: 1910, Girl at party—$500

Serving tray: 1913, Signed by Hamilton King—
$1,000

Trays

Serving tray: 1913, Oval—$800

Serving tray: 1914, Large oval—$850

Serving tray: 1914, Betty—$800

Serving tray: 1916, Elaine—$500

Serving tray: 1920, Garden girl—$975

Serving tray: 1920, Large oval—$1,000

Trays

Serving tray: 1922, Summer girl—$900

Serving tray: 1923, Flapper girl—$500

Serving tray: 1921, Autumn girl—$1,000

Serving tray: 1924, Smiling girl—$950

Serving tray: 1926, Sports couple—$875

Serving tray: 1927, Curb service—$800

Serving tray: 1927, Girl with bobbed hair—$775

Serving tray: 1928, Soda fountain clerk—$775

Serving tray: 1929, Girl in swimsuit holding glass—
$525

Serving tray: 1929, Girl in swimsuit holding bottle—
$525

Serving tray: 1930, Bathing beauty—$660

Serving tray: 1930, Girl with a telephone—$475

Serving tray: 1931, Farm boy with dog—$940

Serving tray: 1932, Bathing beauty—$810

Serving tray: 1933, Francis Dee—$625

Serving tray: 1934, Maureen O'Sullivan—$950

Serving tray: 1935, Madge Evans—$440

Serving tray: 1936, Hostess—$450

Serving tray: 1937, Running girl—$360

Serving tray: 1938, Girl in the afternoon—$280

Serving tray: 1939, Springboard girl—$310

Serving tray: 1940, Sailor girl—$325

Serving tray: 1941, Girl ice skater—$345

Serving tray: 1942, Two girls at car—$370

Serving tray: 1953, Same tray in French—$100

Serving tray: 1953, Girl with menu—$85

Serving tray: 1950s, Girl with wind in her hair—$100

Serving tray: 1957, Birdhouse tray—$200

Serving tray: 1957, Girl with the umbrella—$325

Serving tray: 1957, Rooster tray—$150

Serving tray: 1961, Pansy garden, Be Really Refreshed—$35

Serving tray: 1961, Pansy garden, Coke Refreshes You Best—$35

Serving tray: 1968, Lillian Russell—$60

Serving tray: 1968, Lillian Russell, same tray in French—$60

Serving tray: 1969, Lillian Nordica—$35

Serving tray: 1971, 1909 reproduction—$5

TV Trays

Item	Value
1956, TV tray	$20.00
1958, TV tray picnic basket	$75.00
1961, TV tray	$15.00
1962, TV tray	$15.00

1956, TV tray—$20

1958, TV tray picnic basket—$75

1961, TV tray—$15

1962, TV tray—$15

Vienna Art Plates (1908-1912)

In 1905, the Vienna Art Company made a variety of plates advertising bakeries, taverns, haberdasheries and Coca-Cola. The metal plates had very ornate frames and were packed in wooden, velvet-lined cases. The Western Coca-Cola Bottling Company used Vienna Art plates for advertising instead of the conventional Coke trays. The Chicago-based company, a subsidiary of Coca-Cola, provided syrup and advertising items to bottlers within its territory. As Coke memorabilia, these trays are valuable simply because of the stamp on the back.

Vienna Art Plates found with original ornate gold frame can be worth as much as 50% more. These plates can be found with no advertising on the back. Reverse side reads: "Vienna Art Plates PAT. FEB. 21st 1905 Western Coca-Cola Bottling Company Chicago, Ill."

Item	Value
1905	$500.00
1905	$475.00
1905	$450.00
1905	$425.00
1905	$400.00
1905	$400.00
1905	$450.00
1905	$425.00
1908, "Topless" tray	$5,500.00
1908, "Topless" art plate	$900.00
1908-1912	$600.00
1915, Distributor Signs	$550.00
1915, Distributor Signs	$575.00

Vienna art plate: 1905—$500

Vienna art plate: 1905—$475

Vienna art plate: 1905—$450

Vienna art plate: 1905—$425

Vienna art plate: 1905—$400

Vienna art plate: 1905—$400

Vienna Art Plates

Vienna art plate: 1905—$450

Vienna art plate: 1905—$425

Vienna art plate: 1908, "Topless" tray—$5,500

Vienna art plate: 1908, "Topless" art plate—$900

Vienna Art Plates

Vienna art plate: 1908-1912—$600

Vienna art plate: 1915, Distributor Signs—$575

Vienna art plate: 1915, Distributor Signs—$550

Wallets

Leather items are precious and very collectible. Gold leaf was used for embossing and gives the wallets a rich look. In the 1920s, the size of our currency changed from large bills to small bills. This change, in turn, effected the size of wallets.

Item	Value
1907, Engraved coin purse	$200.00
1910, Two-sided coin purse	$200.00
1906, Embossed coin purse	$200.00
1910, Change purse	$155.00
1912, Billfold	$90.00
1912, Change purse	$300.00
1915, Billfold	$250.00
1918, Wallet with calendar	$100.00
1919, Wallet	$90.00
1920s, Embossed with bottle	$50.00
1928, Billfold	$35.00
1928, Embossed	$75.00
1936, 50th Anniversary pocket secretary, leather	$150.00
1940s, Key case	$125.00
1950s, 50th Anniversary "Coca-Cola Bottling Company," in box	$75.00
1960s, Telephone book	$15.00
1960s, Key case	$15.00
1970, Wallet	$50.00

1907, Engraved coin purse—$200

1910, Two-sided coin purse—$200

1906, Embossed coin purse—$200

1910, Change purse—$155

1912, Billfold—$90

1915, Billfold—$250

1918, Wallet with calendar—$100

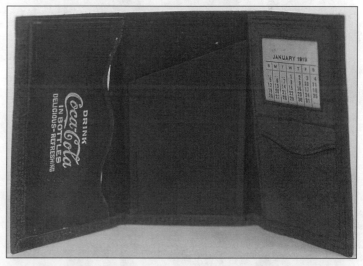

1919, Wallet—$90

1920s, Embossed with bottle—$50

1928, Embossed—$75

1940s, Key case—$125

1970, Wallet—$50

Watch Fobs

Watch fobs are connected to a leather strap with a pocket watch attached to the end. The watch was then placed in the pocket and the watch fob hangs on the outside of the pocket.

Item   Value

1905, Celluloid, "Drink Coca-Cola in Bottles" ..$1,000.00
1905, Celluloid, girl with flowers $1,000.00
1907, Brass with silver (on back), "Drink Coca-Cola in Bottles 5c" $175.00
1908 ....$200.00
1909, Brass $300.00
1910, Brass with gold (on back), "Drink Coca-Cola Sold Everywhere 5c" $250.00
1910, Celluloid (on back), "Drink Coca-Cola in Bottles 5c" $1,000.00
1911, Celluloid (on back), "Drink Coca-Cola in Bottles 5c" $800.00
1912, Celluloid, 1-1/2" diameter $2,500.00
1917, "Drink Coca-Cola in Bottles" $225.00
1920, Swastika, brass $200.00
1920, Swastika $200.00
1920, Brass with red enamel, "Drink Coca-Cola in Bottles" $150.00
1920s, Bulldogs, 1-1/4" x 1-1/4" "Coca-Cola, Delicious and Refreshing" on back $175.00
1920s, Bulldogs, 1-1/2" x 1", without Coca-Cola on front $200.00

Watch fob: 1905, celluloid, "Drink Coca-Cola in Bottles"—$1,000

Watch fob: 1905, celluloid, girl with flowers—$1,000

Watch fob: 1907, brass with silver (on back), "Drink Coca-Cola in Bottles 5c"—$175

Watch fob: front and back,
1910—$250

Watch fob: 1907, brass with gold (on back), "Drink
Coca-Cola Sold Everywhere 5c"—$175

Watch fob: 1909, brass—$300

Watch fob: 1910—$250

Watch fob: 1910, celluloid (on back), "Drink Coca-Cola in Bottles 5c"— $1,000

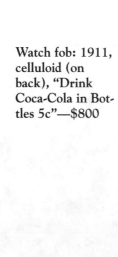

Watch fob: 1911, celluloid (on back), "Drink Coca-Cola in Bottles 5c"—$800

Watch fob: 1912, celluloid, 1-1/2" diameter—$2,500

Watch fob: 1917, "Drink Coca-Cola in Bottles"—$225

Watch fob: 1920, swastika, brass—$200

Watch fob: 1920s, bulldogs, 1-1/2" x 1", without Coca-Cola on front—$200

Watch fob: 1920, brass with red enamel, "Drink Coca-Cola in Bottles"—$150

Watch fob: 1920s, bulldogs, 1-1/4" x 1-1/4" "Coca-Cola, Delicious and Refreshing" on back $175

Watch fob: 1920, swastika—$200

Appendix

Chronology of Coca-Cola

1886	Coca-Cola is created in Atlanta by Dr. John Pemberton.
1886	First Coca-Cola ad placed in the *Atlanta Journal*.
1888	Asa Candler purchases Coca-Cola after Pemberton's death.
1891	Asa Candler buys complete control of Coca-Cola.
1892	Asa Candler and associates form the Coca-Cola Company.
1893	The trademark "Coca-Cola" is registered with the United States Patent Office.
1894	Joseph Biedenharn puts Coke in bottles for the first time.
1895	Coca-Cola is sold throughout the United States.
1899	The first bottling plant opens in Chattanooga, Tenn.
1905	Straight-sided bottled with the new crown cork is used.
1915	Roor Glass Company of Indiana creates the contour bottle designed from a drawing of a coca pod.
1915	The hobbleskirt bottle first patented.
1916	The 6-1/2 oz. bottle approved and used by bottlers.
1919	The Coca-Cola Company is sold to Trust Company.
1923	The six-bottle cardboard carton is introduced.
1929	The bell-shaped glass is unveiled.
1933	First full-color ad in *National Geographic*.
1933	The automatic fountain dispenser is displayed at World's Fair.
1940	Coca-Cola is bottled in 45 countries.
1943	Eisenhower requests bottling plants overseas.
1944	Billion gallons manufactured.
1945	Coke registers as a trademark.
1951	*Time* magazine features Coke on its cover.
1953	Two billion gallons manufactured.
1955	King sized bottles are introduced.
1955	Flat-top steel cans are produced for the military.
1959	Three billion gallons manufactured.
1960	Fanta is introduced.
1960	The Coca-Cola Company purchases Minute Maid.
1961	Sprite is introduced.
1963	Tab is introduced.
1963	Four billion gallons manufactured.
1966	Five billion gallons manufactured.
1969	Six million gallons manufactured.
1971	Seven million gallons manufactured.
1972	Mr. Pibb is introduced.
1974	Sugar-free Sprite is introduced.
1978	Plastic PET bottles are introduced.
1979	Mello Yellow and Ramblin Root Beer introduced.
1982	Diet Coke is introduced.
1982	Coca-Cola purchases Columbia Pictures.
1983	Tab, Diet Coke and caffeine-free Diet Coke are introduced.
1984	Diet Fanta introduced.
1985	Coca-Cola Classic and Cherry Coke were introduced.
1985	New Coke was introduced.
1985	Coca-Cola was the first soft drink to land aboard the space shuttle Challenger.
Present	More than 685 million servings of Coca-Cola products are consumed each and every day worldwide. Coca-Cola is available in 195 countries and appears in over 80 different languages.

Source Directory

Internet Sites

Bobby Liao has the most complete site with links to everything Coca-Cola—*http://xenon.stanford.edu/~liao/cokewww.html*

The Soda Fountain has great information and links to everywhere, also—*sodafountain.com*

Cocaman and Cocababe's Vintage Coca-Cola Advertising Antiques has something for everyone—*http://www.angelfire.com/oh/cocacolaantiques/index.html*

Pop Central is Alan Petretti's site and is full of constantly updated information—*nostalgiapubs.com/index.html*

Places to Visit

The World of Coca-Cola
55 Martin Luther King Jr. Dr.
Atlanta, GA 30303-3505
(406) 676-5151
A wonderful exhibit with more than 1,000 articles of memorabilia, as well as soda fountain displays and films from the past. A must for any Coke collector visiting the Atlanta area.

Biedenharn Candy Company and Museum of Coca-Cola Memorabilia
1107 Washington St.
Vicksburg, MS 39180
(601) 638-6514
This great piece of history was restored in 1979 to its original 1890 appearance. There is easy access to four museums, the Vicksburg National Military Park, shops, restaurants and casinos. The Vicksburg Foundation for Historic Preservation, a not-for-profit corporation, owns and operates this authentically restored candy store and museum.

Wonderful World of Coca-Cola
3785 Las Vegas Blvd.
Las Vegas, NV
(702) 270-5953
You don't have to be next door at the MGM Grand Hotel to see the 100-foot tall Coca-Cola bottle lighting up the strip. The 12,000-square-foot super store offers a delightful visit into the past with plenty of amusement and goodies to buy. Along with the history, there are numerous exhibits and displays.

The Schmidt Museum of Coca-Cola
1201 North Dixie
Elizabethtown, KY 42702
This extraordinary museum is located inside of the Coca-Cola Bottling of Company of Elizabethtown, Ky. Features the largest collection of memorabilia in the world. My parents sold most of their collection to Bill and Jan, which brought them some one-of-a-kind items.

National Club

The Coca-Cola Collector's Club
P.O. Box 49166
Atlanta, GA 30359-1166
http://www.cocacolaclub.org/
A good group with over 7,000 members, monthly newsletter, annual convention. The members meet regularly to trade and sell their collectibles, auctions, swap meets and the popular room-hops. The club also publishes a monthly newsletter for the members. A non-profit organization, not affiliated with the Coca-Cola Company.

Publications

The Enjoyer
Henk van Suffelen
Hogerhorst 105
6714 LD Ede The Netherlands
   A bi-monthly magazine for Coca-Cola fanatics

De Blikvanger
Blik op Blik
c/o Gerritt Walet
Pinksterbloem 54 1689 RC Zwaag
The Netherlands
   Quarterly newsletter of the can collector's club

Books

Classic Soda Machines by Jeff Walters, 1995, Memory Lane Publishing, P.O. Box 2290, Pollock Pines, CA 95726

Coca-Cola Price Guide, by Al and Helen Wilson (Schiffer, 1994)

Coca-Cola Trays, by William McClintock, (Schiffer, 1996)

Coca-Cola Trays from Mexico and Canada, by Marty and Don Weinberger

Coca-Cola: A Collector's Guide to New and Vintage Coca-Cola Memorabilia, by Randy Schaeffer and Bill Bateman, C.C. Tray-ders 611 N. Fifth St., Reading, PA 19601

Coca-Cola: A History in Photographs 1930-1969, by Howard Applegate, Voyageur Press, 1996

Coca-Cola: Its Vehicles in Photographs 1930 through 1969, by Howard Applegate, Voyageur Press, 1996

Coca-Cola Heritage: A Photographic History of the Biedenharn Coca-Cola Bottling Business, P. Randolph Mayo

Coke's First Hundred Years and a Look into the Future, Shepherdsville, Ky., Keller International Publishing, 1986

Commemorative Bottle Checklist and Cross Reference Guide, Richard Mix, P.O. Box 558, Marietta, GA 30061, fax (770) 422-5649; email *mixintl@aol.com*, complete listing of over 2,000 commemorative bottles

De Courtivron's Collectible Coca-Cola Toy Trucks: An Identification & Value Guide by Gael Courtivron, Collectors Books

For God, Country and Coca-Cola: The unauthorized history of the great American soft drink and the company that makes it, by Mark Pendergrast, New York: Maxwell Macmillan, 1993; Collier Books, 1994

"Mr. Anonymous" Robert W. Woodruff of Coca-Cola, by Charles Newton Elliott, Cherokee Pub. Co., 1982

Petretti's Coca-Cola Collectible's Price Guide, Antique Trader, 1997

The Real Ones: Four Generations of the First Family of Coca-Cola, Elizabeth Candler Graham, Barricade Books, NJ, 1992

The Schmidt Museum Collection of Coca-Cola Memorabilia, Vol. I, by Bill and Jan Schmidt, Taylor Publishing Co., 1983

Vintage Coca-Cola Machines: A Price and Identification Guide to Collectible Coolers and Machines, by Steve Ebner and Jeff Wright, Fun-Tronics, P.O. Box 3145, Gaithersburg, MD 20885

Books *(out of print/difficult to find)*

Coca-Cola: An Illustrated History, by Pat Watters, New York, Doubleday, 1978

Coca-Cola: Part I: a Refreshing Taste of Americana, by Cecil Munsey, Western Collector 1969

Coca-Cola: Part II: The World's Most Famous Bottle, by Cecil Munsey, Western Collector 1969

Coca-Cola: The First Hundred Years, The Coca-Cola Company, 1986

Collecting Hobbleskirt Coca-Cola Bottles, by William V. Seifert, Carstarphen Publishing Co., 1978

Coca-Cola Collectibles Volumes I-IV, Shelly and Helen Goldstein. (Can be found now and then at antique stores. These books are priceless, not for their prices, but for their beauty. For some, these books are the only opportunity in which they can enjoy viewing such a beautiful and rare collection of old collectibles. The books have always been and still are, collectible.

Golson's Unique and Varied Bottles, by Golson L. Hook

The Illustrated Guide to the Collectibles of Coca-Cola, by Cecil Munsey Hawthorne Books, 1972

Dating by Slogans

An advertising slogan is the easiest way to date an item. Due to advertising standardization, most ads have the same look and offer the same messages. During any specific year, an advertising slogan would appear in almost every medium—blotters, signs, billboards, newspaper and magazine advertisements. The following is a list of slogans used in specific years.

1886
Drink Coca-Cola
Cures Headache, Relieves Exhaustion
Delicious! Refreshing! Exhilarating! Invigorating!
Delicious Refreshing Invigorating

1898
Cures Headache
Rests the Tired Nerves and Brain
At All Soda Fountains
The Best Brain and Nerve Drink

1900
Deliciously Refreshing
For Headache and Exhaustion, Drink Coca-Cola

1902
Drink Carbonated Coca-Cola in Bottles

1904
Delicious and Refreshing
Coca-Cola is a Delightful, Palatable, Healthful Beverage
Coca-Cola Satisfies
Pure and Healthful

1905
Drink a Bottle of Carbonated Coca-Cola
Coca-Cola Revives and Sustains
Drink Coca-Cola at Soda Fountains
The Favorite Drink for Ladies When Thirsty, Weary or Despondent
Good All the Way Down
Flows from Every Fountain
Sold in Bottles

1906
The Drink of Quality
Thirst Quenching—Delicious and Refreshing
The Great National Temperance
The Ideal Beverage for Discriminating People

1907
Delicious Coca-Cola, Sustains, Refreshes, Invigorates
Cooling…Refreshing…Delicious
Coca-Cola is Full of Vim, Vigor and Go—A Happy Drink
Sold Everywhere—5c
Step into the Nearest Place and Ask for a Coca-Cola
The Great International Drink

1908
Sparkling—Harmless as Water, as Crisp as Frost
The Satisfactory Drink
Ask for a Bottle…Sold Everywhere
Coca-Cola is Better, Try It. Wherever Ginger Ale, Seltzer is Good, Coca-Cola is Better, Try It

1909
Delicious, Wholesome, Refreshing
Delicious, Wholesome, Thirst Quenching
Drink Delicious Coca-Cola
Whenever You See an Arrow, Think of Coca-Cola

1910
Drink Bottled Coca-Cola—So Easily Served
It Satisfies
Quenches the Thirst as Nothing Else Can

1911
It's Time to Drink Coca-Cola
Real Satisfaction in Every Glass
The Most Refreshing Drink on Earth

1912
Demand the Genuine—Refuse Substitutes
All the World Loves a Coca-Cola
Ask for It…We Serve the Genuine
Both—Delicious and Refreshing

1913
Ask for It By Its Full Name—Then You Will Get the Genuine
The Best Beverage Under the Sun
It Will Satisfy You
A Welcome Addition to Any Party—Anytime—Anywhere

1914
Demand the Genuine By Full Name
Exhilarating, Refreshing
Nicknames Encourage Substitutions
Pure and Wholesome

1915
The Standard Beverage

1916
Its Fun to Be Thirsty When You Can Get a Coca-Cola
Just One Glass Will Tell You

1917
Three Million a Day
The Taste is the Test of the Coca-Cola Quality
There's a Delicious Freshness to the Flavor of Coca-Cola

1918
Anytime, Everywhere, the Favorite Beverage
Refuse Imitations

1919
Coca-Cola is a Perfect Answer to Thirst That No Imitation Can Satisfy
It Satisfies First
Quality Tells the Difference

1920
Drink Coca-Cola With Soda
The Hit That Saves the Day
The Friendly Hand No Matter Where You Are

1922
Quenching Thirst Everywhere
Thirst Knows No Season
Thirst Can't Be Denied
Thirst Reminds You—Drink Coca-Cola

1923
Refresh Yourself
A Perfect Blend of Pure Products from Nature
There's Nothing Like It When Your Thirst
Always Delightful

1924
Pause and Refresh Yourself
In the Distinctive Bottle
Always a Delightful Surprise
Drink Coca-Cola All Year 'round

1925
The Sociable Drink
Stop at the Red Sign and Refresh Yourself
Six Million a Day
Refreshment Time

1926
Thirst and Taste for Coca-Cola are the Same Thing
Stop at the Red Sign
Pause a Minute—Refresh Yourself

1927
Around the Corner from Anywhere
At the Little Red Sign
Enjoy for Its Purity and Wholesomeness
Pure as Sunlight

1928
A Pure Drink of Natural Flavors
By the Way—Refresh Yourself
Good Taste and Refreshing

1929
The Pause That Refreshes
Enjoy Refreshment and Be Refreshed for Enjoyment
A Great Combination
Ours is Ice Cold

1930
Meet Me at the Soda Fountain
So Refreshing
The Busiest Man in the World (Santa Claus)

1931
Get It Here Ice Cold
Come Up Smiling for a Fresh Start
Every Bottle Sterilized

1932
The Drink That Makes the Pause Refreshing
Ice-Cold Sunshine
It Means So Much—Costs So Little

1933
Don't Wear a Tired Thirsty Face
Bounce Back to Normal
Between Bites

1934
Carry a Smile Back to Work
Ice Cold Coca-Cola is Everywhere Else—It Ought to be in Your Family Refrigerator
When it's Hard to Get Started, Start with a Coca-Cola
The Drink That Awakens Energy

1935
All Trails Lead to Ice-Cold Coca-Cola
The Pause That Brings Friends Together

Coca-Cola—The Pause That Brings Friends Together
Cooling Refreshment

1936
What Refreshment Ought to Be
Get the Feel of Wholesome Refreshment

1937
America's Favorite Moment
So Easy to Serve and So Inexpensive
Stop for a Pause…Go Refreshed

1938
Anytime is the Right Time to Pause and Refresh
At the Red Cooler
The Best Friend Thirst Ever Had
Pure as Sunlight

1939
Make Lunch Time Refreshment Time
Makes Travel More Pleasant
Thirst Stops Here
Coca-Cola Goes Along

1940
The Package That Gets a Welcome at Home
Try It Just Once and You Will Know Why
Bring in Your Thirst and Go Away Without It
The Greatest Pause on Earth

1941
A Stop That Belongs on Your Daily Timetable
One of the Simple Things That Make Living Pleasant
Completely Refreshing
Get Together With Refreshment

1942
The Only Thing Like Coca-Cola is Coca-Cola Itself
Refreshment That Can't Be Duplicated
Wherever You Are, Whatever You Do, Wherever You May Be, When You Think Refreshment, Think Ice-Cold Coca-Cola

1943
The Only Thing Like Coca-Cola is Coca-Cola Itself—It's the Real Thing
That Extra Something
A Taste All Its Own
You Work Better Refreshed

1944
High Sign of Friendship
A Moment on the Sunnyside

1945
Whenever You Hear "Have a Coke," You Hear the Voice of America
Happy Moment of Hospitality
Coke Means Coca-Cola
A Happy Symbol of a Friendly Way of Life

1946
Coca-Cola Gives a Touch of Hospitality to Sociable Moments
As American as Independence Day
The Friendliest Club in the World
Friendliness and Coca-Cola Go Together, Like Bread and Butter

1947
Serving Coca-Cola Serves Hospitality
Relax With the Pause That Refreshes
Come Over for a Coke
Hospitality is in Your Hands

1948
Where There's Coca-Cola There's Hospitality
Think of Lunchtime as Refreshment Time
Coke Belongs
Everybody Likes to Work Refreshed'

1949
Along the Highway to Anywhere

1950
Help Yourself to Refreshment
Good With Food

1951
Good Food and Coca-Cola Just Naturally Go Together
Add Zest to the Hour
You Taste Its Quality

1952
Coke Follows Thirst Everywhere
What You Want is Coke
Be Refreshed
Coke Adds Zest

1953
Dependable as Sunrise
Refreshing Anytime—Anywhere
Work Better Refreshed

1954
For People on the Go
Matchless Flavor
Always a Fresh Delight

1955
Almost Everyone Appreciates the Best
America's Preferred Taste
Brighten Your Meals With Coke

1956
Feel the Difference
Make Good Things Taste Better
Bring Home the Coke
Enjoy the Quality Taste

1957
Sign of Good Taste
The Loved Sparkling Drink in All the World
Coke is Just Right
Enjoy the Real Great Taste

1958
Refreshment the Whole World Prefers
The Cold, Crisp Taste of Coke
Cheerful Lift of Coke

1959
Cold, Crisp Taste That Deeply Satisfies
Make It a Real Meal
Be Really Refreshed
Relax Refreshed

1960
Relax With a Coke

Revive With a Coke
Coke Refreshes You Best

1961
Coke and Food—Refreshing New Feeling

1962
Enjoy That Refreshing New Feeling
Coca-Cola Refreshes You Best
Enjoy the Lively Life of Coke

1963
A Chore's Best Friend
Things Go Better With Coke
For the Taste You Never Get Tired Of
Go Better Refreshed

1964
You'll Go Better Refreshed
Coca-Cola Gives That Special Zing—Refreshes Best
Enjoy Coca-Cola With Ice Cream

1965
Something More Than a Soft Drink
Enjoy Coca-Cola
You Trust Its Quality

1966
Coke…After Coke…After Coke
Coca-Cola has the Taste You Never Get Tired Of

1967
Coke is the Taste You Never Get Tired Of

1970
It's the Real Thing
Coke Adds Life to Everything Nice

1971
I'd Like to Buy the World a Coke

1975
Look Up America

1976
Coke Adds Life

1979
Have a Coke and a Smile

1982
Coke is It!

1985
We've Got a Taste for You
America's Real Choice

1986
Catch the Wave
Red, White & You

1989
Can't Beat the Feeling

1990
Can't Beat the Real Thing

1993
Always Coca-Cola

Bibliography

Hoy, Anne. *Coca-Cola: the First Hundred Years*. Los Angeles: George Rice & Sons, 1986

Petretti, Alan. *Petretti's Coca-Cola Collectibles Price Guide*, Dubuque, IA: Antique Trader Books, 1997

Schaeffer, Randy and Bill Bateman. *Coca-Cola, a Collector's Guide to New and VintageCoca-Cola Memorabilia*. Philadelphia, PA: Running Press Publishers, 1995

Wilson, Helen and Al. *Coca-Cola Price Guide*. Atglen, PA: Schiffer Publishing Ltd., 1997

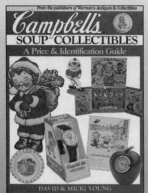
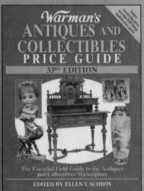

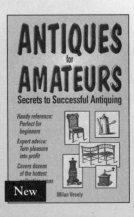

OUR PRICING EXPERTS HAVE DONE ALL THE WORK
SO YOU CAN HAVE ALL THE FUN!